7-55-68

OBSTACLES TO DEVELOPMENT

OBSTACLES
TO
DEVELOPMENT

---

by
LAUCHLIN CURRIE

MICHIGAN STATE UNIVERSITY PRESS
EAST LANSING
1967

★
　★
★
　★
　★

Contents

Foreword   vii

I. The Nature of the Problem   1

II. Development Goals and Strategies   18

III. The Relevancy of Development Economics to Development   30

IV. Development and the Decline of Competition   48

V. Population and Development   63

VI. Technology and the Problem of the Mix in Underdeveloped Countries   80

VII. Disguised Unemployment and Saving-Investment   90

VIII. Underdevelopment and Foreign Trade and Exchange Policy   103

IX. Mobility, Employment and Output: Interacting Elements in a Theory of Development   120

X. Why Foreign Aid?   129

Foreword

This book is a collection of papers presented to various audiences while I was a visiting professor at Michigan State University during the fall term of 1965, or were inspired by the stimulating discussions I had with members of the class "800 V" at that time. They are all related to the broad theme of underdevelopment and, addressed to different audiences, unavoidably entail some duplication. While I regret this, I have found, as a teacher, that ideas that are to a certain degree novel must generally be presented in different forms and in different contexts if they are to have any impact.

While these papers contain suggestions of a positive nature they all stress the obstacles that stand in the way of development so that the title of the collection is not inappropriate, though it may convey a false impression of inclusiveness, since the obstacles I have singled out are, in my judgment, the most important and do not constitute an exhaustive list. Various chapters supplement or develop the ideas expressed in my book *Accelerating Development* (McGraw-Hill Book Co., 1966).

I am most appreciative of the opportunity afforded me by the Economics Department of Michigan State University to conduct a graduate course in development and to the Departments of Economics at Wisconsin, Illinois, Cornell, Harvard and M.I.T. for their invitations to give lectures or participate in conferences.

LAUCHLIN CURRIE

OBSTACLES TO DEVELOPMENT

I

The Nature of the Problem

Since some of you are not economists, I decided to talk about the more dynamic aspects of development that touch upon the subject matter of a number of disciplines. These are generally messy problems that do not lend themselves to algebraic or even diagrammatic treatment—a type of exposition that the present day economists strangely like to refer to as elegant—and for that reason among others are usually neglected. Nevertheless, they are tremendously important and horribly difficult because they must in part be treated in qualitative rather than quantitative terms and an adequate treatment takes us far beyond the confines of any single discipline, even extending to fields such as psychiatry, law, morality and religion. When you stop to think of it, this is not surprising, as the word "development" embraces the whole life of a people in its various manifestations and interreactions. Even inserting the qualifying word "economic" before development does not enable us to escape from a consideration of the influence of non-economic factors, if we want our treatment to be realistic and accurate.

In addition to the difficulty of dealing with a number of variables are the difficulties of the time element involved, the general unreliability of quantitative data and the impossibility of controlled verification and experimentation. Many things are happening at once, some cause and some effect and some both cause and effect. We can make very little use of the economic theorists' favorite device of impounding most of these variables in a box called "other things being equal," or of refined methodology. We can make use of simple basic economic concepts, a limited use of quantitative data carefully checked for "reasonableness," relatively simple statistical techniques, some knowledge of thinking in related fields and a big dose of something which, for want of a more precise term, I will call good judgment. This, I admit, is not very satisfactory but we must do the best we can with what is by far and away the most important problem of our time.

For those of you who are not economists or at least my kind of economist let me first devote a moment to the nature of the problem of development.

Breaking the problem down I will first consider the objective or goal. This is too frequently treated simply as a matter of food —of staving off hunger and eventually famine—which unfortunately it is dangerously close to in parts of the Far East. But for most countries this is still much too constricted a characterization of the objective. Merely to stay alive is hardly an ideal or worthy objective of development. What we would wish for all people is first and foremost the diminution of pain, suffering, fear and insecurity—all components of what I like to call "ill-fare"—so far as man's present knowledge makes this possible. Secondly, on the more positive side, we would wish the widespread diffusion of a modicum of goods and services well above the bare minimum required to remove pain and suffering. Next would come education, diversions and tolerable working conditions. And close behind or even with my third step would come what a distinguished economist has referred to as an enhancement in the quality of living. We may differ on the elements of a better quality but I think we would also find, at least in an academic community, a large measure of agreement.

Most economists agree on a division of the countries of the world into developed and underdeveloped categories, though they may not always agree on the basis of the division. In any case, all the so-called developed countries have more or less attained the first three objectives mentioned and are at least worrying about and discussing the fourth. No one of the so-called underdeveloped countries has attained a satisfactory degree of any of the elements of a desirable society, except for a small proportion of their peoples.

The problem of development is made up, to my mind, of the problem of explaining this divergence and working out the means of attaining our four-fold objective—in medical terms, making the correct diagnosis and prescribing the appropriate remedy to attain a condition of health.

Let me now take up the diagnosis, which will involve us immediately in the complex causal interactions of social phenomena. Instead of starting with the controversial and, to many of you, unfamiliar diagnosis of underdevelopment, let us start with something more familiar and less controversial—the nature of the benign circle of self-generating growth in which the United States now happily finds itself.

The attainment of greatly reduced "illfare" and of positive satisfaction from a bountiful and widely diffused supply of goods and services requires, as a first approximation, two things—high physical output per capita and a fair measure of equality of income, wealth and opportunity; in other words, a pie big in relation to the population and an equitable sharing of the pie. The United States has the largest production per capita in the world; in the equitable sharing of this production it has made much progress but is still considerably behind the Northern European countries.

Turning to the first element, it is not difficult to see the self-generating forces or benign circle at work. A high standard of living makes possible prolonged education, a massive research and investigation effort, and large sums available for investment. The growth of the market makes possible a high degree of specialization and the attainment of more and more economies of large scale production. Millions of consequent scientific advances, inventions, improvements and organizational changes result in higher output or increased leisure per worker or a higher standard of living. Advances in agricultural techniques and productivity make it possible for two percent of the working force to produce seventy-five percent of the agricultural production. Advances in industrial productivity make for a steadily increasing output of goods with less workers. Advances in both make possible a steadily rising percentage of the active population in services, including education. And what about the strictly non-economic elements in the process?

A highly complex economic organization demands a people who will abide by the rules of the game, who are, on the whole, punctual, reliable and possess good work habits. The cultural inheritance of Americans was favorable to development, and development in turn has strengthened those elements in the inheritance that are favorable to development. As standards of education and responsibility rose in the private sector, higher standards of competence and responsibility were required in the public sector, which in turn reacted favorably on the economy and diminished waste in public investment.

Up to fairly recently, the rise in economic and educational levels led directly to a fall in birth rates. The consequent decline in rates of population growth—to 1.4 percent per annum from 1900 to 1950 despite the heavy immigration at the beginning of the period—meant the attainment of a more favorable rate of dependents per worker and the maintenance of a favorable rate of population to resources.

Finally, the high and rising standards of income and education had repercussions in a variety of other fields such as the quality of the law enforcement agencies and the judiciary, diversions, and conservation. Americans became a much more law abiding people. There is clearly still a national nostalgia for the far off time where it is at least assumed that one could with impunity beat a person to the draw or sock him in the jaw but a widespread indulgence in these pastimes is clearly not compatible with the maintenance and progress of a complex civilization.

This, of course, is a highly abbreviated treatment of a complicated process, but I hope it will serve to illustrate the self-perpetuating character of the growth in developed countries. No aspect of life is left untouched by the process. There is a constant interplay of economic, political and cultural forces. When the process did not itself directly bring about a more equitable distribution of income, it did so indirectly through progressive income and inheritance taxes and the development of social legislation—both of which would have been inconceivable in a simpler time when free land and only modest fortunes precluded such politically induced remedies. Even so, it must be admitted that war played a part in accustoming the rich to high rates of taxation and that otherwise the struggle would have been longer drawn out.

Developed countries, assured that self-generating growth is at work and only needs occasional adjustments, can take time off to concentrate on those areas where it is felt the economic system is not giving the desired results—such as a space program or the abolition of the hard core of poverty or improving the quality of living, where there is an evident lag.

The study of the most spectacular failures of the benign circle —the long drawn out existence of an extremely poor rural cotton economy up until 1940 and of Appalachia up until today and the more recent vicious circle of continuing poverty and crime in the larger cities—are most instructive for the diagnosis of the problem in underdeveloped countries. These countries, of course, differ widely among themselves but they all have one thing in common, the existence of vicious circles or interacting causal sequences that impose continuing obstacles to development. The following remarks apply in particular to most Latin American countries where natural resources are still abundant in relation to population, where industrialization has a good base and yet where, by the standards of developed countries, an abnormally large proportion of the people eke out a very poor living from the land.

They are all characterized by a high birth rate, a falling death rate and a rate of population increase three times or more higher than that of most developed countries. While there are many very poor in the cities and their numbers are growing, the bulk of the poverty is concentrated in the rural regions among the small farmers. All these countries have a common predominant cultural background.

Whatever may be the condition in the Far East, where population appears to be already pressing on natural resources, the explanation of backwardness in Latin American countries cannot be found in inadequate natural resources, and hence must be considered as man-made.

The first clue that comes to mind is the abnormally high rate of population growth of three percent per annum and over. This means that the population is doubling every twenty-three years or so. The population explosion in Latin America is due almost entirely to falling mortality rates, especially infantile. In developed countries, as the mortality rate fell, so also did the natality rate. We may cite the timing of the fall in the death rate and the consequent sharp rise in the rate of population growth as a major difference between the problems of development in the currently developed countries in their earlier stages and the underdeveloped countries of today. Paradoxically enough, a case can be made for the claim that science and technology have to date worsened the lot of the majority of people in the world.

And now I come to the second link in a causal sequence. There appears to be a good deal of empirical evidence to the effect that high birth rates are closely associated with low economic and educational levels. In other words, the governing factor appears to be not the availability of birth control information nor religious influences but rather such things as feelings of responsibility, foresight and ambition. This is particularly true in rural regions in underdeveloped countries where the incentives to restrain births are very weak. In the rural tropics living space is no problem and clothing little more. Children can pick up a living from a bountiful nature and climate at an early age and actually contribute to the family's needs as well as furnish the only kind of invalidity and old age insurance available. A bare subsistence is easy but to gain more in rural regions is extraordinarily difficult.

So you can begin to see the circle forming—a very large, poor and ignorant rural population—increasingly high birth rates— falling death rates—continued poverty and continued lack of education. Many of the younger people—some through induction in the army and police, some through domestic service and some merely in search of work—go to the cities, but not enough to prevent the rural population from continuing to increase in absolute terms. In other words there can be a very sizeable migration to the cities and still an increase in the rural population.

At least, you may object, the increase in population—particularly the urban part—means increased demand for food and fibres, rising prices for such products and hence relatively rising income for farmers. But here, at least in Latin America, enters again the science and technique of developed countries. The increased demand is met by mechanized farming, which requires much less land and labor, so relative agricultural prices and hence the real income of peasant farmers do not rise.

But at least, you may say, the condition of the rapidly growing urban sector rises. This is only in part true as those of you who have read of the poverty in Mexico City, told in Oscar Lewis' *Children of Sánchez*, will appreciate. To explain why this is so, I must here introduce additional elements that characterize Latin American countries. One is a very high degree of inequality in income and opportunity. One study on Perú maintains that one quarter of one percent of the families receive thirty-five percent of the national income. I cannot vouch for the accuracy of this, but it is certain that incomes and buying power are very unequally distributed. In relatively wealthy Venezuela, Professor Shoup of Columbia University found that forty-three percent of the population at the bottom received only ten percent of the income.

There is also another kind of inequality—that between the organized urban workers, perhaps ten percent or less of the total, and the ninety percent unorganized and/or self-employed peasants. This may easily be of the order of eight or ten to one when all fringe benefits are included. Note that trade unions, generous labor codes and high social security benefits have been taken over from the advanced or developed countries, but long before attaining the degree of development and equality of income those countries possess. Moreover, they are unavailable for the overwhelming majority of the people. Instead of condemning this type of inequality, northern liberals praise it.

The economic significance of these different forms of inequality is that they act both to prevent the growth in the mass market for consumer goods necessary for very rapid development of industry and the creation of jobs for the annual addition to the labor force and migrations from the countryside. The economic system is not functioning as it did in the United States in the nineteenth century when competition both in industry and labor was strong and widespread and where the growth in the mass market for consumer goods encouraged a rapid growth in industry and a corresponding growth in jobs in those industries and in complementary activities. The result is that while there is migration and movement of workers in underdeveloped countries there is not nearly sufficient mobility, in the sense of a mechanism to transfer workers to better paying jobs, to begin to cope with the magnitude of the problem. Neither did the nature of the exports and the export policy in most of the Latin American underdeveloped countries remedy the deficiency in better paying jobs and yield sufficient exchange, although this is too big a theme to explore here.

I have been stressing economic and demographic factors. But obviously an adequate explanation must go deeper. The cultural inheritance, for instance, was and is not nearly as favorable for development as was the northern culture. From purely an economic point of view, perhaps the most important aspect of the cultural inheritance of Latin America is its individualism. The individual and his family group confront a hostile world. There is little of the sense of being one's brothers' keeper. It is difficult to arrive at a consensus. It is difficult to enforce discipline or for individuals to subordinate their personal interests to the general good. Political parties are dominated by the personality cult. In Colombia political leadership is even sometimes passed on from father to son, with issues being secondary. The cooperative movement has had hard going in this uncongenial environment. Other facets of this dominant cultural characteristic are a tendency not to abide by the rules of the game and to resort to direct action. Both driving a car and refereeing a game are hazardous occupations. A more serious manifestation is the impotence of democratic institutions such as Congress. The tendency to resort to direct action is particularly disastrous in the field of economic policy where hasty improvisation is the rule. Generalized solutions of problems are likely to be shelved while thousands of individuals try through influence and other means to work out individual solutions for themselves.

Northern writers often write as though the privileged class is aware of and united in defence of its privileges. Perhaps I do not have the proper perspective, but I fail to see that unity but rather a continual jockeying for power and the readiness to espouse measures actually inimical to the immediate and direct interests of the upper class in order to gain or retain power. On the whole, the well-to-do classes are as ignorant of the inner functioning of the system of free enterprise as are the exploited.

The point of all this for present purposes is to illustrate another vicious circle. The economic system is functioning badly. Hasty and ill considered interventions are therefore resorted to and the system functions even more badly and so on. The malfunctioning of the economic machine results in widespread impatience and sense of frustration, in a decline in the prestige of governments, whether democratic or authoritarian, in a resort to direct action (civic or student strikes, robbery, violence, etc.) and a consequent continued malfunctioning of the system.

Still another vicious chain of interacting sequences can be found in the relation of poverty, inequality and resentment to declining morality—insecurity of life and property—growing reliance on repression through use of the army and police—more resentment and further deterioration in ethical values—loss of confidence—flight of capital—faulty functioning of the economic system—and still more poverty for more people.

In short, the benign circles at work that I outlined for developed countries are replaced by a host of interacting vicious circles in underdeveloped countries that make the transition from the latter to the former type of economy infinitely difficult. The most noteworthy transformation, that of Japan, was facilitated, contrary to popular belief, by a relatively low rate of population growth—1.3 percent per annum for the period 1900-1950—and above all by a cultural inheritance highly favorable to development.

The problem of development, in short, is infinitely more complex and difficult than is commonly assumed and the current attack on the problem is woefully inadequate. In any case, I would stress the nature of these self-generating and continuing causal sequences as the main difference between developed and underdeveloped countries. No attack upon the problem of underdevelopment that fails to break the primary vicious circle of poverty (particularly rural)—high birth rates and population growth rates—ignorance and indifference—and poverty again— can hope to succeed. A growth in the gross national product per capita is of little consequence if it fails to touch the condition of the great mass of the poor or to break the vicious circles I have been stressing.

I have come to think that possibly the most important and yet most difficult problem confronting planners in underdeveloped countries is to determine the nature of the problem. Or putting it differently, there are too many apparently unrelated problems which result in a dispersion not only of physical resources in attempts at partial, piecemeal solutions, but also in a dispersion of mental efforts. A conscientious reading of the daily press in Latin American countries is not only an exhausting but also a frustrating task leaving one frequently hopeless and bewildered. It appears impossible to bring order out of the chaos or to establish priorities in the urgency of problems or to devise a program that will resolve a number of the apparently unrelated problems at the same time. And yet, I am convinced, this is what must be done, and done first.

It has become the custom to assume that the increase in the volume of goods and services per capita is the given goal or objective of policy in underdeveloped countries. This, for instance, is the only goal or objective set forth in the original Alliance for Progress declaration and in countless other publications. The North Americans, however, felt uneasy about this as an exclusive goal, and added a second—the more equal distribution of income —which they hoped to secure by changes in land tenancy and taxation reform. For various reasons, however, inequality as between propertied classes and workers, and between urban organized workers and the rural self-employed, appears to have grown rather than decreased since the Alliance was started.

It is not difficult to point out the inadequacy of the attainment of a given rate of increase in the gross product as a national objective and the possibility that this could be consistent with the worsening of the condition of over half the people, if inequality is great and growing.

On the other hand, the multiplicity of current major problems in the economic field dictates the necessity of synthesis—of trying to establish priorities, of regrouping the problems as primary or derivative. Otherwise, in sheer desperation, we are driven back to the increase in the gross product as the all encompassing problem. In order to illustrate my point, I am going to tax your patience by listing briefly the economic problems encountered in a casual reading of the daily press in Colombia together with some others whose existence is hardly realized.

(1) The agrarian problem. Under this head I would include the persistent low standard of well-being of over half the population in rural regions and in small towns dependent on agriculture, in terms of incomes, health, education and diversions and in comparison to rising urban standards.

(2) The problem of great and growing inequality, as between propertied classes and workers, and as between urban and organized workers and the rural self-employed.

(3) The problem of how to accelerate mechanization and technification in agriculture without causing even more misery and suffering among rural workers.

(4) The problem of arresting and reversing the growth in the numbers of peasants and squatters.

(5) The problem of land erosion and destruction of natural resources.

(6) The problem of growing insecurity of life and property in rural regions.

(7) The problem of providing prolonged and obligatory primary education for a growing proportion of the children and of increasing opportunity to obtain secondary and university education.

(8) The problem of raising health standards, especially in rural areas.

(9) The problem posed by one of the highest growth rates in population in the world.

(10) The problem of providing remunerative employment for a three percent net addition to the working force each year.

(11) The problems of growth of the larger cities (public services, housing, traffic, etc.).

(12) The problem of preserving for agriculture in Colombia the limited areas of level land at altitudes of 2,600 and at 1,000 meters.

(13) The problem of how to secure a higher rate of industrialization.

(14) The problem of inadequate foreign exchange which in turn can be broken down into a number of other problems (borrowing, exports, exchange rates, etc.).

(15) The problem of improving the efficiency of public administration.

(16) The problems that will arise in the future from the lack of a national urban policy.

(17) The problem of how to avoid continuing fiscal deficits.
(18) The problem of how to prevent chronic inflation.

Some of these problems overlap but on the other hand many can be broken down into major components and the list extended still further.

Actually, in Latin American countries at the moment, there are no specific, coordinated programs to attain either a given rate of growth in the gross product or indeed any other overall objective. Different government entities and individuals are attempting to resolve, in some manner or another, separately but at the same time, most of the problems I listed and many others I did not list. Such lack of coordination must inevitably accentuate existing problems and create new ones. For example, wholesale tax exemptions to encourage industry, agriculture, exports, housing, etc., have completely eroded the base of direct taxes in Colombia and have contributed to budgetary deficits and inflation. In short, it would seem most unlikely that an attempt to resolve many problems simultaneously without coordinated action or reference to a basic plan can be very successful. It is my personal view that it is the particular task and responsibility of the economist to define national objectives, to urge priorities, to show the inter-relation of apparently unrelated problems, to devise consistent, non-contradictory programs to achieve specified objectives. Why the economist? Because, presumably, we are the only ones who have some idea of how the system functions, of the inter-relationships, of the theory of incidence and of the need of priorities. The political leaders have, of course, the final responsibility for making decisions but in my view economists have the privilege and the obligation to advise.

Accepting this challenge, though I hope in a spirit of humility, let us take another look at our list of problems and see if we cannot bring some order out of apparent chaos. Let us, for the moment, give top priority to the solution of the agrarian problem which I will state perhaps dogmatically to be that of too low income for most people in the rural areas. This top priority is based on various grounds—because over half the people are involved, because they are the poorest half and because the vicious circle I have been stressing is peculiarly concentrated in rural regions.

Raising the standard of living of the current rural population to that of urban workers would resolve a number of the other problems listed. In order to show why this is so, I have to anticipate the nature of the solution I proposed for Colombia, which consists of the creation of remunerative jobs producing things the people need, including additional food-stuffs, urban housing and public services, and fabricated articles of mass consumption. My point is to indicate how the choice of an objective, say the creation of 700,000 urban jobs in three years, and the achievement of this objective, would affect our range of problems.

The increased well-being of the countrymen, both those who secure more remunerative employment and those who remain in rural regions, and remunerative employment for the natural addition to the labor force, would clearly provide an impetus to agricultural mechanization and technification, would augment the real demand for industrial products, would reduce the inequality between urban and rural workers, would mean the abandonment of some marginal lands and uneconomic-sized holdings. It would be a contribution to the conservation of natural resources, and would, especially in the cities, give more children better education and health. The immediate effect on the rate of population increase is less certain, as the tendency for the urban birth rate to fall well below the rural might be offset for a time by a further decline in infant mortality. Over the longer run, it appears fairly certain that industrialization and urbanization would dampen down the population explosion. Again, the effect on insecurity of life and property is uncertain though I should imagine that fewer and more prosperous countrymen and the opportunity of securing better paying jobs in the cities would contribute to the solution of the problem.

Thus, of our initial list of eighteen national problems, the solution or even partial solution of the agrarian problem would help at the same time to resolve eleven. Of the remaining seven problems, three center around urban growth, where it must be admitted the problems would be accentuated by our solution of the agrarian problem. For this reason, I devoted some hundred pages of a study I directed on the growth problems of Bogotá to the elaboration of an urban policy for Colombia that seeks to secure balanced urban development and avoid gigantism, to secure greater densities with less congestion, that would permit a general upgrading in housing, would reduce transport costs and would save the Sabana de Bogotá and the Valle del Cauca for agriculture for future generations.

This leaves us then with four familiar problems. The one that would be accentuated would be the chronic shortage of foreign exchange. To resolve this, I would try to relate the borrowing program to the attainment of the specific objectives I mentioned, to expand exports of primary and other products to the world in general and plan for a major increase in trade. In this respect agreement with the Government of Venezuela for studies on economic integration opens up promising possibilities of, among other things, securing more capital goods in exchange for consumer's goods, to the benefit of both countries.

So far as I can see, the only additional and new problem that would be raised would be that of financing the program, which, more than anything else, is a question of institutional arrangements designed to mobilize and divert resources from less urgent to more urgent uses and from less to more intensive utilization. Fortunately, for those of you who are economists, I do not have to convince you that from a technical point of view, the real limitations on a program such as I am suggesting are, as in war, physical rather than financial, though, of course, the financing may encounter political obstacles.

In any case, the point I wish to make here is that by a proper statement of the problem, diagnosis and choice of means, we can bring some order out of apparent chaos, can reduce rather than augment the number of unrelated problems, and can give drive, purpose and cohesion to national planning. The broad lines of the program are familiar to all economists—the achievement of industrialization and urbanization through manpower released by the technification of agriculture, and capital goods gained by borrowing and exports. The novelty lies only in the ways and means proposed to accelerate this familiar cycle that all advanced countries have experienced. There is little scope for experimentation in economics. But we can observe and analyze and, as I have attempted to demonstrate, synthesize and arrive at generalizations that provide explanations and solutions of apparently unrelated problems. In this way, we can play a positive role in molding our environment to improve the well-being of the people.

Let me now illustrate my point in a negative fashion by restating our principal problem as being, not as before, too low rural incomes, but rather, as has been done, inadequate agricultural production. Immediately the nature and emphasis of the indicated programs changes. What is now indicated is a program of more agricultural workers, more investment, more credit, more irrigation projects, roads and so on. If the program succeeds, production will increase beyond demand at current prices, prices will fall, city dwellers will spend less on agricultural products, and agricultural incomes will fall. As a consequence, mechanization will be discouraged, small holdings increased, fertility will be decreased, and erosion and the destruction of resources will grow. With lower agricultural income, the problems of rural education, health, morality and personal and property security will become more acute. The national birth rate would remain high under these conditions and the problem of providing other than a subsistence living for the net annual addition of the labor force becomes more difficult.

In other words, if our diagnosis is mistaken, we will be farther than ever away from a solution of our main underlying problem. This hard truth may be concealed for a time by the salt cellar or sprinkler approach—a little for all. If, however, you ask yourself what would happen if we were to make a major effort to increase agricultural production by a major additional investment in roads, reclamation projects, colonization and parcelization and diversification projects, rural education and so on, I think you will see the point. Our program of development would end up by intensifying our problems.

With more of our resources channeled into rural spending, less would be available for urban housing and public services which in turn means more slums and less adequate public services. If, by chance, we should succeed in obtaining a major increase in physical agricultural production, the hard reality of economics would hit back at us in the form of unremunerative prices and incomes and unsold stocks of goods.

But, you may object, the creation of many more urban jobs will *require* more agricultural production and this in turn requires increased investment. Quite true, but in this case the production and investment will be in *response* to an increase in effective demand. It is the increased investment in agriculture *divorced from any prior increase in demand* that I am objecting to. And please bear in mind the group of countries I am discussing.

I have been at pains to insist that, as professionals concerned with development, we have a responsibility to regroup and restate our multiple problems to render them susceptible of being tackled in a single comprehensive program, that such a program must follow from a correct diagnosis and a proper statement of objectives and that, finally, we need a deliberately accelerated period of growth in order to be sure that our take-off is self-generating and not unwinding. I regret to have to say that up to now we do not share agreement on the nature of the problem, the objective or objectives of a program, the strategy to be used, or finally on the urgency of the problem—all of which at this state constitutes a parlous and shocking state of affairs and indicates how infinitely more difficult are the problems of economics and politics than are those of the natural sciences.

II

Development Goals and Strategies

In the previous chapter I was mainly concerned with the nature of the problem of underdevelopment and with ultimate goals of policy. I propose here to turn to more immediate goals and strategies.

Here we enter into what the New Yorker would call The Department of Utter Confusion. Underdeveloped countries are swarming with missions and technicians, all concerned with different problems and different prescriptions. Individual governments and planning agencies are all too often behaving like firefighting departments, rushing to put out one fire after another. The metaphor is not exact, as most of the fires are set by the governments themselves. There is an unbelievable babel of diagnoses and prescriptions. Improvisations follow improvisations and the economic organization becomes almost impossible to understand. It is extraordinarily difficult to carry out a calm analysis, to put first things first, to work out a consistent national plan that makes sense, or to secure any consensus on that plan.

It may help in understanding the source of the confusion to distinguish between the individual project approach and the overall national approach, though these are not in watertight compartments. Generally, however, the Agency for International

18

Development, the International Bank and its affiliates, the Interamerican Bank, the Export-Import Bank, and the private foundations are concerned with the financing of individual projects, though some of these have on occasion exerted pressure for changes in national fiscal or exchange policies. They have added a little to available exchange, to gross investment and have, in some cases, improved the management and financing of certain public entities. I think they would admit, however, that whatever constructive influence they have been able to exert is scarcely discernible in the broad sweep of events.

The agencies associated with the United Nations and certain semi-public and private groups have been more concerned with giving advice on specific projects and programs and also with guidance on national planning. As I said, it is dangerous to make too sharp a distinction, as the Alliance for Progress also talks about planning and agrarian reforms. The Food and Agriculture Organization thinks it knows what the agrarian problem is, the Ford Foundation is financing the Harvard Economic Advisory Group and demographic studies in Colombia, the Economic Commission for Latin America (affiliate of the United Nations) has aided in drafting national economic plans, both the World Bank and the Committee of Nine of the Alliance have evaluated national plans and so on.

As you can imagine, to make generalizations in this field is hazardous. However, while exceptions can always be cited, an impressionistic picture which would not be too far from the truth would be that the field of overall national planning, so far as it exists, has been dominated by the United Nations and its affiliates. It has, in my view, been a type of planning of a particularly inappropriate nature. What appears to have happened is that the Keynesian concepts and terminology, originally useful to explain the persistence of mass unemployment in developed societies and to provide a particularly satisfying refutation of that particular fallacy of composition that has to do with individual and aggregate saving, and the theoretical relation, in money terms, of an increase in investment to an increase in income, were adopted for use in dealing with the problems of development of underdeveloped countries. About the same time, largely in the 1950's, economists became disillusioned with welfare and enamoured with quantifying and measuring, Keynesian terminology was given quantitative content both in money and real terms, and saving, investment and gross product were extended to cover government operations. Growth in per capita gross product was explicitly or implicitly accepted as a measure of growth or development (these terms are used interchangeably) and implicitly identified with increased well-being. The resultant violence to concepts and straight thinking in all this was blithely consigned to a file labelled "conceptual difficulties" and promptly forgotten.

This is perhaps an exaggerated picture and there are many notable exceptions among economists but in the hands of the less expert or less cautious technicians, the consequences of this process become really ridiculous. Thus in the Ten Year Plan for Colombia, worked out by ECLA technicians, government accounts were divided into investment and operating expenditures (which I assume correspond to consumption but the technicians did not quite dare to say so). A propensity to save was calculated, which in turn gave a multiplier. Programmed public "investment" and assumed increases in private investment were worked out and added together and a capital-product ratio calculated. Since this did not meet the arbitrarily chosen goal of an increase of 2.6 percent in gross product per capita, a final assumption had to be made of decrease in the capital-gross product ratio on the existing stock of capital. All money figures were then deflated to arrive at "real" terms.

You can either call this playing house or development made simple by definitions and arithmetic, but in any case it seems to me to have nothing whatever to do with the basic problems or with the intractable vicious circles of underdevelopment. But, I regret to say, missions from both the World Bank and Committee of Nine did not question the basic approach and were only concerned with changing the arithmetic. The same happened with the Venezuelan National Plan and, I assume, other plans.

In a slightly more sophisticated and hence more dangerous form it is the basic approach to development set forth first by Ragner Nurske and Jan Tinbergen and then incorporated in the highly influential book of the United Nations called *Programming Techniques,* where everything is subordinated to the Fundamental Equation of Growth. These, and ECLA's *Introduction to Programming,* are the texts of hundreds of young economists in underdeveloped countries, many of whom, I again regret to say, were trained in American universities. Despite the complete fiasco of the Colombian Plan, the distinction between public "investment" and "operating" expenses remains embedded in the law and, worse still, in the minds of cabinet ministers and financial writers. The simple formula for development is still to increase the former and reduce the latter.

Let me digress for a moment to mention a curious thing that happened to me in the writing of my last book on development. I was struck by a remark of Keynes to the effect that "the difficulty lies, not in the new ideas, but in escaping from the old ones, which ramify, for those brought up as most of us have been, into every corner of our minds" and decided to quote it in the frontispiece of my book. It was only much later, in going over the final proofs, that I realized that with the passage of time the old ideas I was attacking derived in part from the Keynesian or neo-Keynesian approaches of thirty and fifteen years ago! These are the ideas that have now ramified into every corner of our minds and from which, I venture to suggest, we must try to escape when we turn to Latin American underdeveloped countries. The quotation itself, however, is still a most apt one, and, as I said, Keynes himself was concerned with escaping from still older and more primitive ideas, and cannot be blamed for the excesses of his followers.

Probably, you will object, the approach may have been abused by the programmers but this does not offset its basic soundness. By increasing saving we increase capital formation which in turn gives rise to a growth in real production. By borrowing abroad, we further increase capital formation and the G.N.P. Deflating

money production to arrive at real output and dividing by the
increase in population are standard procedures.

I have made various criticisms of this line of thinking. Basically
they come down to the point that it is more applicable to developed economies where the basic assumptions of a free enterprise society are still relatively valid, where income is less
inequably divided, and statistics are more reliable. But it is
precisely in those societies that the goals and programming techniques described are least used. In the conditions of 1932-33, for
example, what was called for was not an increase in saving but
an increase in consumption, obtained by creating jobs or, in short,
by an increase in aggregate effective demand. In wiping out the
remaining pockets of poverty, reliance is not on the trickle down
theory or on simple division to get comfortable average per capita
results. In dealing with chronic unemployment, reliance is on the
combination of increasing aggregate demand and restraints on
sellers' inflation. Even in dealing with balance of payment difficulties, resort is to direct measures.

In attaining the truly fantastic production results of World
War Two, we did not start by increasing saving but by organizing
to meet what then appeared to be impossible goals of war time
production. Similiarly, in rebuilding the capital equipment of
Europe after the war, under the Marshall Plan, we resorted to
specific goals.

American economists and political administrators, interested in
policy, may take some pride in the great economic accomplish-
ments of this generation. However, improving the plight of nearly
two-thirds of the world's population—the greatest task and challenge of all—is not one of these. Here the record is one of growing
failure. Most of the American effort, as I said, is going into individual projects; most of the overall planning is inspired by
agencies who have nothing to loan and have reduced planning
to simple definitions and simple arithmetic.

This is all the more distressing since, if I may be pardoned the
phrase, more sophisticated economists are agreed that capital formation is only one of the factors, and not the most important, that

influences growth of product; that there is no predictable relation between an increase in capital and an increase in gross product; that the bulk of capital formation follows a growth of product rather than precedes it; and that there are different possible goals to be attacked by different measures. For example, Professor Domar wrote in 1957 that capital accumulation "is more an effect—almost a symptom—rather than a primary cause [of economic growth]."[1] Various other writers, such as Solow and Kendrich, have minimized the role of capital in contrast with that of technical progress, which among other things, includes *improvements* in capital. The developed world is teeming with technical knowledge, some of it appropriate and some inappropriate, that is available to the underdeveloped world as soon as the latter organizes itself to take full advantage of that which is appropriate.

The more immediate goal is to put the vast army of unemployed to work by creating new jobs in fields other than agriculture. This, however, requires in turn energetic action to prevent the beginning of an increase in effective demand from being offset and nullified by sellers' inflation. A further step is to prevent the gross and growing inequality in incomes from finding expression in increased demand by the wealthy for the consumers' goods and services, and the capital goods to make such goods and services. While truly effective action to modify the pattern of income distribution is the result only of a long struggle, something more immediate to modify the pattern of *consumption* of the wealthy to prevent it from absorbing an excessive share of the growth in production can be done by invoking war time types of control over construction, investment and imports. As Professor Galbraith has said, in underdeveloped countries we need a new theory of consumption.[2] It is much easier to prevent the wealthy from spending increased income than it is to prevent them from getting it or to take away an increased share of what they already

---

[1] Evsey Domar, *Essays in the Theory of Economic Growth* (New York: Oxford University Press, 1957), p. 12.

[2] J. K. Galbraith, Lectures on Development, Harvard University Press, 1962, pp. 43-53.

have. Similarly it is easier (though not easy) to keep the remuneration of the strongly organized industrial workers from increasing in excess of the growth in per capita income than it is to ask them to accept a lower real wage.

Since, with the Ruggleses and Viner, I believe high birth rates to be more a result of poverty than of lack of birth control knowledge or the attitude of the Catholic Church, I find the enemy to be mass poverty resulting from mass unemployment. Given high rural birth rates, sellers' and monetary inflation and gross inequality of income, the capital formation approach and the accompanying trickle down theory cannot break this circle. While I would not for a moment oppose other lines of attack as supplementary ones—exhortations and birth control clinics for example—I am afraid that they will be comparatively ineffective, especially as long as poverty and high birth rates are concentrated in rural areas.

A most laudable objective, you may reply, but hardly practicable and, after all, we have to be realistic. At least that is the response I have received in official quarters in Colombia. It is reminiscent of the reaction to sensible proposals from 1930 on to 1939, where we were confronted with the same problems, though in less degree, of mass unemployment, sellers' inflation and a breakdown in the mechanism of resource allocation.

I have tried to meet this objection, without much success, by resort to analogies. One is the Great Depression and the New Deal, relying on Professor Galbraith's assertion that all economists today are satisfied that the New Deal approach was the correct one. It failed only in being too small and too timid and not recognizing the extent of the leakages. Another is the Second World War which supplied Roosevelt with a valid excuse to be economically "unsound," to set tremendous goals and to subordinate everything to meeting these goals. It is the Second World War, also, that provides us with an analogy of the superiority of the "pull" over the "push" factor in labor mobility in supplying a breakthrough in the rural South that ended a 150 year vicious circle of poverty —ignorance—high birth rate—poverty—discouragement of agricultural mechanization—low physical productivity—and poverty again. Still another analogy was the brilliant success of the Marshall Plan when the United States underwrote import requirements while Western Europe rebuilt its productive plant—another striking example of what can be done by a correct diagnosis of the problem, setting correct goals, concentration of effort, and tailoring the strategy to achieve the overriding goals.

These analogies suggest that the problem of underdevelopment should be met by marshalling and concentrating resources to provide new jobs outside of agriculture, by developing an incomes and price policy to prevent the increase in demand for wage goods from being stultified by increases in industrial incomes and prices, by aiming deliberately at a rapid and massive increase in consumption (including housing and urban public services), a more intensive utilization of capital goods and the infrastructure to provide more consumer goods, by discouragement, for the time being, of luxury spending and more capital intensive and more roundabout methods of production (on the analogy of the resource allocation mechanism in the Second World War), by adopting an urban policy that will permit more people to walk to and from their work, and by locating markets and schools nearer homes in the larger cities, and providing for new plants to be located in smaller cities where the costs of public services and urban transport can be kept down. No development that looks toward suburban living and mass ownership and operation of private motorcars should be tolerated in what are still what Simon Patten called "pain economies."

What happens to the Gross National Product, both gross and per capita, can be left for the statisticians to calculate later. Our goals are a massive non-agricultural job program, a reduction in the numbers and a rise in the well-being of the agricultural population, less inequality and a big rise in consumption of what used to be called wage goods, a fall in birth rates and eventually a fall in population growth rates.

Before these goals and strategies are dismissed as being impractical, I would ask you to contrast them with the actual goals and strategies. These latter are concerned in large part with a host of individual projects—with power plants, roads, land reclamation, housing, partially free food and a few balance of payments loans and loans for general purposes. There is no general staff to establish priorities. The criteria may be profitability as determined by cost-benefit studies, "social" purposes, incentives to secure a devaluation or a rise in taxes, the financing of exports from particular countries, getting rid of surplus food, and frequently little more than can be characterized as preferences and prejudices of lenders. There is no assurance that such a hodge podge program can yield any rational pattern of priorities of effort and investment. In terms of total investment the combined aid and loan program may amount to anywhere from one percent or less up to ten percent—hardly enough to affect significantly the total.

When we turn to the so-called national plans we find that they again form a hodge podge of goals, strategies or just plain activities. The overall goal is a rise in something called the gross national product per capita—a series of such inaccuracies as to be practically useless (see Oskar Morgenstern *On the Accuracy of Economic Observation*) and available only long after the event. As a national objective it is especially worthless in underdeveloped countries because of the wide and probably growing difference in income levels concealed by an average per capita figure. Finally, it does not lend itself as an objective of planning as there is no direct and predictable relation between anything the state controls and the gross product per capita. The state controls only directly that part of "investment" that probably has the least predictable relation to gross output. For the rest, it "influences" and "encourages" private investment (but it may equally not affect nor encourage such investment). In short, most national plans of underdeveloped countries are based on a complete misconception of the nature of the problem. Hence, the goals and the strategies are largely erroneous or at least irrelevant to the solution of the basic and primary problem. The objective of a rise in gross product per capita is a red herring distracting attention from the lack of purposeful planning. It permits a wide, heterogenous and frequently mutually contradictory range of activities to be included in the "plan." There are countries whose vicious circles have long since reached the crisis stage demanding heroic action but who are still going through the motions of drawing up plans for a rise in the G.N.P.

In contrast, all I propose is that we first try to arrive at agreement on the nature of the problem and its causes, and base our immediate and longer term objectives and strategy on our findings. The only criticism I have come to accept as being valid, both from my experience in the Great Depression and more recently in an underdeveloped country, is that mentioned by Keynes "the difficulty lies, not in the new ideas, but in escaping from the old ones." A society that had the economic sophistication and dedication to accept and pursue such a program as I propose would not be underdeveloped. You will recall my descriptions of the numerous vicious circles in which underdeveloped countries find themselves. I think the emblem that could be appropriately placed on all their flags is the Laocoon. For an underdeveloped country to break all its vicious circles unaided would be truly a boot-strap operation which we have little reason to expect. To do this in the face of the opposition or disapproval of the world lending agencies is almost inconceivable except in the case of a Castro-type government that had nothing to lose from the disapproval of such agencies.

So finally I come to your responsibility as economists and as Americans. The only alternative to a Castro-type solution with its immediate retrogression and at least temporary suffering may be for the leading economists in the leading universities and international agencies to work out a new Marshall Plan based on a correct diagnosis, an adequate strategy and a concentration of effort over a sustained period, and the application of this plan to a willing and apt pilot country. I mention a pilot operation because we need, I think, a demonstration effect before we can apply the remedy wholesale.

Would it be worth the effort? That I must leave to you to

decide. Joan Robinson argues that economics is still nationalistic and economists, nationalists. That may very well be true. Yet, even on a narrowly nationalistic basis I do not think you can look forward with equanimity to a world described by Raymond Frost as one in which "less than half of the world may be living in a slick, clean and immensely prosperous industrial civilization, while the majority remain shut in a vast agricultural slum."[3] Geometric progression in population is just hitting its stride. Dr. Sen, Director of F.A.O. calculates the population of under-developed countries in thirty-five years at four-fifths the world's population, if present rates of population growth continue. At a certain point, which is already being reached in some countries, the almost forgotten law of diminishing returns may very well overtake the economies of scale and technical progress. If first seventy percent, then eighty percent, then ninety percent of the world's population live in a vast agricultural slum, what are you going to do? Occupy them to put out the inevitable fires? Build Berlin Walls around yourselves not to keep people in but to keep people out? Even professional people in a little poor country like Colombia are finding that they can do better for themselves in the United States. I am told that there are 20,000 requests for permanent visas for residence in the United States pending in Colombia alone. The pressure to enter any part of the developed world from all parts of the underdeveloped will rise with every year.

I do not want to be labelled as an economic terrorist, but quite sincerely I think a crisis is building up. Another chain reaction that may help to bring on the crisis is the present world wide drive on the part of developed countries to increase their exports and decrease their imports. The vicious interrelation of economic, cultural and political developments of an adverse nature appears to be in an accelerating phase. It cannot be bought off indefinitely by more and more loans for specific projects or to bolster falling exchanges. These loans will shortly require wholesale re-

3 Raymond Frost, *The Backward Society* (New York: St. Martin's Press, Inc., 1961), p. 14.

financing on more and more favorable terms. With every day that passes the problem is more difficult of solution.

Since I started talking along these lines in 1961, the situation has sensibly deteriorated in Colombia and, I believe, other Latin American countries. There is, in Colombia, disillusionment with the results of the Alliance for Progress, of Agrarian Reform, of planning and of the Latin American Free Trade Association. The prestige of democratic political institutions has declined and we are living [1965] under what appears to be a permanent state of siege. Personal and property insecurity, especially in the countryside, has reached a point where agricultural land is no longer an attractive investment and may threaten the growth in commercial-type farming. The actual situation differs from country to country but I do not think that it can honestly be said that any are replacing their vicious circles by purposeful control over their economic environment.

In short, in the supreme economic and social problem of our time, it appears to me that economists are failing, especially in the United States, to give a clear lead. This is a grave charge but I think it can be substantiated by any critical and objective analysis. It is still not too late, but time is running out. I can only hope, for the sake of literally billions of people, that economists will rise to the challenge of their time. The peoples of developed economies have gained a large measure of control over their individual economic environments; over the infinitely more important environment of the world as a whole, there is at present a complete and utter lack of control.

III

*The Relevancy of Development Economics to Development**

What I am about to say I should like to characterize as a tentative hypothesis applying certainly not to all economists in this field but rather to certain tendencies I seem to detect. The literature on development is so enormous that I have been able to do no more than sample it. I have relied particularly on a few recent texts and collections of readings in the hope that their authors and editors have been able to cover much more of the literature than I have been able to do. Even in these, however, there are considerable divergencies. The applicability of my generalizations, therefore, may well be more limited than I think.

Let me first try to gain a little perspective by relating a personal experience. When, in 1949, I was asked to organize and direct the first study mission of the World Bank there were no precedents for a mission of this sort and indeed nothing called development economics. I just assumed that it was a case of applying various branches of economics to the problems of a specific country, and

* This paper touches on some subjects already treated in this collection, but from the point of view of university teaching of the subject of development.

accordingly I recruited a group of specialists in public finance, foreign exchange, transport, agriculture and so on. I did, however, include some engineers and public health technicians. What emerged was a series of recommendations in a variety of fields. I was at pains to entitle it "the basis of a program" rather than a socio-economic plan. However, after the publication of the report and my return to Colombia and my work as adviser to a non-partisan committee of distinguished citizens appointed to study the report, I had great hopes that something like an over-all plan might emerge in which the Bank would finance the exchange cost of certain projects in transport, power, and so on, if the Colombian Government would agree to finance certain pro-grams in health, education and public administration and adopt certain fiscal reforms. At a critical moment, however, the Bank shied away from this proposal and limited itself to projects in the transport and power fields. This was a fateful decision as it set the pattern for the Bank's lending operations, with slight depar-tures and modifications, up to the present time. The Bank became a bank in a rather narrow sense of the term, instead of a true economic development institution that would participate in and finance a country's overall plan of development, and in this course it was followed by other lending agencies.

It is interesting to note that although at that time I was reason-ably familiar with Keynes' *General Theory*, I apparently consid-ered that his analysis had little applicability to an underdeveloped country. A little earlier, however, Professors Roy Harrod and Evsey Domar had independently adopted or extended the Keynes-ian analysis to what is now called the theory of growth, and a little later Ragner Nurske had identified growth with develop-ment and had set forth, in a somewhat uncompromising form, the key role of saving and investment in growth and/or develop-ment. At the same time technicians in national accounts had extended the Keynesian concepts of saving and investment to government accounts, national accounts became the chief subject matter of macroeconomics and no country, no matter how under-developed, could afford not to have quantitative estimates of its national accounts. The Gross National Product became (and still is) the single most frequently cited datum of economics. Thus the stage was being set for the elaboration of a new field of "development economics" which intermingled with and overlapped another field called the theory or the economics of growth, which was applicable to all economies. Since "growth" was identified with the percentage rate of increase of one economic series, that of gross output per capita, so also did the test of "development" increasingly become the rate of increase in the product (gross or net) per capita. What one might naively think of as a means to an end became an end in itself.

This process did not occur without protests. Many writers still continue to insist that the distribution of income is as important as its volume, and stress the role of institutional, demographic and cultural factors. However, there appears to be something similar to a Gresham's Law operating in modern economics whereby measurable concepts drive out unmeasurable. As requirements for the Ph.D. degree are modified to screen out all those not possessing considerable natural mathematical ability we may expect this process to continue, until the pendulum again swings back (I hope). Until it does, however, we may expect increasingly to find the basic concepts of older economic theory relegated to elementary undergraduate courses, when the students are usually too young and uninterested to grasp their significance, while graduate training is increasingly concerned with methodology—models and statistical and mathematical techniques undoubtedly indispensable for the solution of certain problems in highly developed economies but for the most part far removed from man and his work, frustrations and satisfactions, particularly in underdeveloped economies.

Consequences of these tendencies can be grasped by glancing through some of the recent literature on development. The objective of development policy is almost universally taken to be a rapid rate of growth in income or gross output per capita. As long as the growth in this series exceeds the rate of increase in population, it is assumed that the country is "developing" or "making progress." The criterion of success in development thus is measured by, as I remarked before, the rate of increase in a particular series.

A second consequence is that the large and generally very arid and abstract literature on "growth" in developed economies, or the pure theory of growth, is taken over bodily and incorporated in what is being called "development economics." Thus we are treated to seemingly endless discussions on varying combinations of factors, on the relation of investment to output, on the utilization and allocation of resources—in fact to everything that one can think of that might affect the gross national output. As you see, this opens up a tremendous field and one can easily fill two or three hundred pages in a very learned and abstract discussion of numerous possibilities. One can then throw in a chapter or so on institutional and possibly even cultural factors (e.g. the tradition-bound peasant clinging to his primitive ways) and something on population growth and land reform and you have your book on development economics.

At this point you may object, what is wrong with that? What is wrong, I think, is that it leaves both government agencies and the student badly equipped to grapple effectively with the policy problems of a specific underdeveloped country. The gap between the precision of the classroom and the messy reality is too great. If he is a foreign student, he is naturally tempted, on his return to his country, to turn from the reality, where he finds his training of little help, to the classroom, where it is, and the process becomes self-perpetuating. Let me try to substantiate these rather sweeping assertions.

First, on the G.N.P. as an objective and measure, the student may or may not have read Oskar Morgenstern's strictures on the insurmountable conceptual difficulties and the inaccuracy of the American G.N.P. and the practical worthlessness of the series in underdeveloped countries.[1] If he has, whatever doubts he may have had are promptly dissipated by the oft repeated statement

[1] Oskar Morgenstern, *On the Accuracy of Economic Observations* (Princeton: Princeton University Press, 1963), pp. 242-282.

that appears to admit these defects but adds, "nevertheless, it is the best measure of growth available" and by the intercountry comparisons of per capita income repeatedly published by the United Nations, which convey a totally misleading impression of exactitude. How can a student be expected to question ninety-nine percent of the leading authorities?

In a country like Colombia, there are *no* statistics for substantial sectors or parts of sectors. For such sectors the gross product is largely estimated or guessed at, so to fix a goal of 2.6 percent per annum in per capita gross income is to adapt a goal which in reality cannot be verified. Moreover, the estimate, when it does appear, is usually at least two years late and is subject to revision for years thereafter. I cannot understand the writers who concede that certain data are virtually worthless but argue that since they are the best we have, we have to use them, and shortly find themselves attributing significance to a change of a percentage point in the series. For example, if the G.N.P. rises three percent it indicates stagnation; if four percent, growth. This, of course, is nonsense.

However, my quarrel with the gross product as a goal and measure of development goes deeper than this. It goes to the very nature of the problem of development. Curiously enough, there is no agreement as to the nature of the problem of development, which is another illustration of the current neglect of basic concepts. One would think that this question must be answered before one dared to write a book on the subject of development but, more often than not, the nature of the problem is implicitly assumed to be simply poverty. Certainly poverty is a pervasive element in all or most underdeveloped countries. But also are many other factors. If we are to pass to the policy field, we must probe deeper into the causes of poverty before we can determine our near term goals and appropriate strategies.

For example, one of the characteristics of underdevelopment is that it displays itself in a multitude of forms. Unless one has thought long and hard on the subject and has tried to distinguish the primary from the secondary problems, the causal from the derivative phenomena, one is likely to be lost and bewildered.

Apparently urgent problems face one at every turn, all crying for attention and action. One group will insist that the key factor is the low level of public administration, another health problems, another education, another the provision of the infra-structure of social capital, another the need for exports or an improvement in the terms of trade, another agrarian reform, another housing, another exchange rate policy, another inflation, another population growth and food production, still another inadequate saving and so on. There is hardly a sector of the economy where serious problems do not exist, or where improvements or reforms do not suggest themselves. Each sector has its advocates asking for technical assistance and money. But obviously to tackle a hundred or more problems simultaneously with limited resources represents a horrible dispersion of effort and waste motion. We must try to separate the primary from the secondary; to put on one side those problems whose solutions await the solution of more basic problems and to concentrate on those basic problems.

It is understandable why an economist who tries to keep his head in such a situation, and is not diverted by the constant succession of monetary, fiscal and exchange crises, decides that the key element is poverty. At this point, however, his conditioning in growth or development economics is likely to suggest that the most effective weapon to achieve "growth" is capital formation, whether borrowed from abroad or created internally. Since he is a product of the Keynesian era he appreciates that capital formation must be matched by saving. This probably explains why his initial natural repugnance to marked inequality in income is blunted, since he feels that such inequality is a regrettable but a necessary condition or price to be paid for saving. Moreover, since he can influence only indirectly investment in the private sector, he is tempted to advocate an increase in "investment" in a controlled public sector financed, as far as possible, by external borrowing. At this point, if he is conscientious, he becomes aware of the appalling waste and lack of adequate criteria in investment in the public sector and is likely to find himself quickly immersed in individual project evaluations.

Again, you may object, what is wrong in all this? My answer

must be that it is a wrong strategy resulting from an inadequate diagnosis. To my mind, the single most important factor differentiating underdeveloped from developed countries is the presence of self-perpetuating sequences or circles generating or maintaining poverty in the former case, and self-generating forces tending to reduce or eliminate poverty in the latter. No diagnosis that ignores this profound difference can possibly, except by accident, suggest the correct strategy. The first task, therefore, of courses or of books on development would seem to be to concentrate on the differences, whether of kind or degree, that distinguish developed from underdeveloped economies. This, in turn, requires a careful study of the causes of abject and continuing poverty of a large proportion of the people of underdeveloped countries. It will quickly be found that in large part the poverty is concentrated in the rural population, that a large percentage of the population is rural, that the birth rate is treble or more the rate in most developed countries while the death rate is steadily falling, and finally that a high degree of inequality in wealth, income and opportunity exists not only between the property owners and workers but also between the organized urban workers and the self-employed peasants. Why these factors persist in underdeveloped countries and have ceased to exist, or have been greatly diminished, in developed countries, in turn requires explanation and will eventually take us into cultural differences, in which we as economists and as products of a particular culture, must tread warily. However, if we hope to say something really meaningful on development or to be practitioners in the field of policy we cannot ignore such matters. For instance, what Oscar Lewis calls the "culture of poverty" may be a much more important tool of analysis than differential calculus.

To lump all these factors contributing to an explanation of the persistence of poverty among the majority of the population into inadequate investment and saving and to confine the measurement of development to the growth of output per capita is, to my mind, to omit a good part of the relevant subject matter and to include a lot of irrelevant material. A recent text on development economics declares at the outset that the distribution of income has normative implications that are outside the context of the argument. However, two pages later the emphasis on output per capita is defended by the claim that the only way to eliminate mass poverty is by growth, and normative concepts are blandly slipped into the statement that growth makes poverty less of a burden and less degrading to the human spirit. If ever there was a value-loaded word it is "degrading."

Actually, reliance is here implicitly placed on the "trickle down theory." But for income and opportunity to trickle down from the top to the bottom a lot of conditions are necessary that characteristically do not exist in underdeveloped countries. Mexico, for example, has during and since the Second World War enjoyed a reported rate of growth in per capita output far outstripping almost all other underdeveloped and even developed countries and yet, apparently, none of this has yet trickled down to the peasants or even, according to Oscar Lewis, to a substantial number of the population of Mexico City itself. In Colombia, about which I can speak with more assurance, there is considerable evidence that not only has inequality grown but that the condition of the peasant has worsened and there are more and more people in this category. In Venezuela, the country people have benefitted little, if at all, from the relatively enormous revenues arising from oil exports and the high reported rate of growth in output per capita. The persistence of a hard core of poverty in the United States—the richest country of the world—is yet another case.

While many economists have discussed various characteristics of underdeveloped countries, including population growth, distribution of income, inflation, terms of trade and so forth, almost all, without much or any discussion, have accepted the rate of growth in production per capita as the objective and measure of success. A notable exception is Jacob Viner, who fifteen years ago wrote "Were I to insist, however, that the reduction of mass poverty be made a crucial test of the realization of economic development, I would be separating myself from the whole body of literature in this field."[2] So far as I know, at least up to the time of my recent book, this proposed alternative was never discussed nor adopted as an objective, possibly because the insidious persistence of the trickle down theory prevented other economists from recognizing that Viner was actually proposing a criterion of development radically different from output per capita. I hasten to add that Galbraith, in his lectures on economic development published in 1962, suggested the need to seek out and concentrate on key strategic factors and of a new theory of consumption for underdeveloped countries in which priority would be accorded production of what used to be referred to as wage goods. I regret that I did not credit him with these suggestions in my current book as unfortunately I only recently had an opportunity to read his stimulating lectures. As his suggestions were expressed in easily understandable prose, probably little attention has been paid to them.

It appears to me that Viner's suggested objective of development—the reduction of mass poverty—is a much more desirable starting point than output per capita, and this for various reasons. In the first place, it directs attention immediately to what should clearly be the ultimate goal of policy and the criterion by which to judge the effectiveness of any economic system. Secondly, it directs attention to the necessity of breaking the vicious circle of poverty—high birth rates—poverty again, which is the most frightening and most difficult barrier in the way of making the transition from the underdeveloped to the developed category. I do not think it can be claimed that any country with a large mass of poverty-stricken peasants and with birth rates of over forty per thousand and whose population is doubling every twenty-three years has assured control of its environment, in any meaningful sense of the phrase. The fact that the attainment of this objective is a tremendous challenge, and certainly requires efforts that dwarf any currently being made, is no valid reason for rejecting it. If that in reality is the nature of the problem, then obviously we must accept it as such, and not pretend that

2 Jacob Viner, *International Trade and Economic Development* (New York: The Free Press of Glencoe, 1950), p. 127.

something very much easier to resolve, at least for some time, is the problem simply because it is easier.

The basic problem, therefore, at least as I see it, on the solution of which the achievement of meaningful control of the environment and the solution of countless other problems depends, is that of breaking the vicious circle of poverty and population growth. I turn to Viner again for a statement of the nature of the problem. "It is a paradox of the population problem that on the ground of historical experience and theoretical analysis the attainment of high levels of per capita income and of education appear to be almost essential prerequisites of a cure of the problem and that the excessive rate of increase of the population is itself the most important barrier to the establishment of these prerequisites."[3] This, again, was written in 1950. You will note that Viner lists as key factors not religious taboos but income and educational levels. This hypothesis was later confirmed for the United States for the period 1890-1940 by a very careful and important investigation by Richard and Nancy Ruggles.[4] The influence of income and educational levels on birth rates far outweighed all other factors. The inverse relationship held even among farmers. According to Ansley Coale, "All countries that have become predominantly urban . . . and now have adult population at least 85% literate have experienced at least a fifty percent decline in fertility."[5]

It is true that after the Second World War the birth rate of the higher income group in the United States moved up and the phenomenon is not yet clearly understood. This later development does not, however, appear relevant to very low income, underdeveloped countries. It is also a fact that the birth rate of the upper income-education group in underdeveloped countries,

[3] *Ibid.*, p. 149.

[4] Richard and Nancy Ruggles, Demographic and Economic Change in Developed Countries; A conference, National Bureau of Economic Research (Princeton: Princeton University Press, 1960), pp. 155-193.

[5] Ansley Coale, Population and Economic Development, The American Assembly, The Population Dilemma, Columbia University (Englewood Cliffs: Prentice-Hall, 1963). Reprinted in *Development and Society,* David Novak & Robert Lekachman (New York: St. Martin's Press, 1964), p. 137.

while falling, still appears to be higher than that of the upper group in developed countries. This, in certain areas, may be in part attributable to religious influence. I suspect, however, that a more plausible explanation may be found in the abundance and cheapness of servants. If so, we may expect to find further declines in the birth rate of this class as servants' wages rise with successful industrial development.

In practically all countries classified as underdeveloped the worst conditions of poverty and illiteracy are concentrated in the very large rural sectors. Hence our major problem becomes that of elevating as quickly as possible the economic and educational levels of rural, village and small town people as well as, of course, the very poor in the large cities. To my mind the agrarian problem is the existence of too low incomes and not of too low production, two entirely different things.

In selecting the goal and the consequent stategy I have laid considerable stress on the necessity of lowering the high birth rate, especially in rural areas. If, however, by some happy chance, the rate should fall substantially for other reasons, as it appears to be doing for the past two years in Communist China and Hungary, I would still defend the goal of alleviating the poverty of the poorest half on the obvious grounds of welfare or, in the conditions prevailing in most underdeveloped countries, of lessening "illfare," i.e., pain and suffering, ill health, insecurity, boredom and the bitter and corrosive elements of envy and hate.

And now I come to the truly desperate urgency of the problem. Again quoting Coale, "The labor force thirty years following the start of a fifty percent reduction in fertility spread evenly over a twenty-five year period is less than ten percent smaller than the labor force resulting from a continuation of unchanged fertility."[6] If we double this period to sixty years, the labor force of Brazil (15 to 64 years of age) "will have increased from 38 million to 161 million."[7] This arithmetic of the problem becomes more frightening with every day the decline in fertility is post-

6 *Ibid.*, p. 136.
7 *Ibid.*, p. 136.

poned. To rely on the natural growth of industrialization, such as occurred in developed countries in the nineteenth century, Coale states, "might take at least thirty to sixty years to attain a state of industrialization that would in itself cause a rapid decline in fertility. In fact, the adverse effects of continuous high fertility in the interim might in itself postpone the attainment of the needed state of advanced industrialization."[8]

The problem is stated in another way by Folke Dovring. Reviewing the process of development in what are now the developed countries, he finds that all, with the exception of the United States, experienced a modest growth rate in population— around one per cent a year—which yields a doubling of the population every seventy-five years or so as contrasted with the twenty-three year doubling period in underdeveloped countries. Non-agricultural employment increased at an annual rate of from 0.7 to 2.7 percent. Doubling the percentage share of non-agricultural employment in the total took a century or more in the early industrialized countries and from fifty to sixty years for the more recently industrialized. Obviously, when the population increase is at the rate of three percent per annum, the growth of non-agricultural employment would have to be extraordinarily high to absorb the increase in the working force and still higher to effect an absolute decline in agricultural employment. Assuming that no such extraordinary growth rates can be expected, Dovring concludes that "There is no reason to expect reduction of absolute numbers in the agricultural population within the near future" and that "It will take decades before agriculture ceases to employ and support the majority of the world's population."[9] But, I may remind you, it is the agricultural section that has the highest birth rates. That is to say, Viner's paradox again and the problem become insoluble.

Harvey Leibenstein,[10] in 1957, stressed the highly significant

8 *Ibid.*, p. 137.
9 Folke Dovring, "The Share of Agriculture in a Growing Population," in Eicher and Witt, *Agriculture in Economic Development* (New York: McGraw-Hill Book Co., 1964), pp. 78-98.
10 Harvey Leibenstein, *Economic Backwardness and Economic Growth* (New York: John Wiley and Sons, 1957), p. 166.

finding that the long term rate of population growth depends very largely on how soon the fertility rate falls following the decline in the mortality rate. In most Latin American countries this so called "fertility lag" is lengthening year by year, thus presaging an extraordinarily high rate of population growth.

In view of these findings it is surprising that many writers on development pay so little attention to the theme. True, the growth in population is almost always mentioned in books on development and it is almost always considered to be excessive, but rarely is it given top priority or treated with a sense of urgency. Generally, the most exercised over the problems are non-economists. As a social science or discipline, we have failed to crack down hard enough on the agronomists, biologists and others who see the problem narrowly in terms of food—of keeping a population with a never ending geometrical rate of growth barely alive.

Why this seeming lack of interest on the part of economists? Is it in harmony with the growth of the non-normative point of view among economists and the conviction that to be "concerned" over anything is to behave as a non-economist? Is it that perhaps unconsciously we do not want to become identified with Malthusianism, a point of view that was long held to be discredited? Or is it because the problem has ceased to be urgent in developed countries and economists are still basically nationalistic in their outlook? Or is it because it is difficult to say anything new on the subject and we have been conditioned to think that we must always strive to be original and to make contributions? Or is it that we have lived too long with the problem and grown a little bored with it? Or is it simply that our imaginations cannot cope with a problem of this magnitude? Or do we think, with Mr. Micawber, that something will turn up and the problem will solve itself through the dissemination of birth control information and a change in the attitude of the Catholic Church? Or perhaps a combination of all these elements?

On the point about birth control knowledge and the attitude of the church, I should like to put in a little warning. Knowledge on how to limit births has been available and has been utilized in developed countries for nearly a century and yet, up to 1940, the Ruggleses found relatively high birth rates in the poor and badly educated groups of the United States whose standards of living and education were nevertheless high relative to the poor of most underdeveloped countries.

When I said that the poverty-excessive birth rate problem is concentrated among the large rural proportion of the population I did not mean that it must necessarily be resolved in the rural areas. On the contrary, I am convinced that it cannot be resolved there. If development implies anything, it implies mechanization and technification of agriculture which in turn implies a drastic reduction in the percentage of the labor force engaged in agriculture. This in turn implies massive shifts in the labor force from agriculture to non-agricultural occupations. The slower the shift the more the population increases, as Coale points out, and the more difficult is a solution of the problem. Hence, paradoxically enough, the solution of the agrarian problem of poverty must be sought in the non-agrarian sectors of the economy of underdeveloped countries.

Actually, in most underdeveloped countries, this shift is occurring, but much too slowly. The cause of the slowness is not only or even mainly, as most writers appear to believe, inadequate saving and investment. In Latin American countries with an infra-structure of social capital and an industrial base, existing capital equipment is, for various reasons, grossly under-utilized and, again for various reasons, the nature of the industrialization process results in too low a ratio of employment to capital. One of these reasons is cost-push or sellers' inflation, familiar to all economists in developed countries. In Colombia, despite substantial foreign borrowing, there appears to have been no rise in industrial employment since the Alliance for Progress began in 1961 to the end of 1965, even though the labor force was growing at the rate of nearly three percent per annum and the population of the larger cities was growing even faster. At the same time there is abundant evidence that real wages and fringe benefits of industrial workers rose substantially in relation to non-industrial earnings and especially peasants' incomes. Rural population continued to increase, although at a slower rate than urban. Some current texts pay little attention to these extremely important tendencies.

Some writers appear to feel that as long as the growth in per capita output is positive, "development" is proceeding and the speed or rate is not too important. William Letwin even lists the view that "rapid" is better than "slow" development as one of four fallacies about economic development.[11] This, I feel, is a grave error, as a slow (and even not so slow) growth in average output per capita may be quite compatible with growing inequality. In any case, as the growth in population continues, the relation of population to natural resources deteriorates; the largest cities begin to encounter rising relative costs for municipal services; impatience, frustration and general economic illiteracy lead inevitably to demagoguery and ill-conceived improvisation; and the prestige both of the free enterprise system and democratic institutions falls.

I hope I am wrong. Having, however, lived in and observed the course of development in a more or less representative country for the past fifteen years, I fear that I am not. The accelerated rate of deterioration during the past four years in the basic elements I have just mentioned is particularly alarming, as it coincides exactly with the period of the Alliance for Progress. The interaction of demographic, economic, social and political elements of a non-constructive nature has been painfully evident. Indeed, it may already be too late to choose different goals and strategies with reasonable chances of success under present systems.

While I do not agree with the economists of the World Food and Agriculture Organization in their exclusive preoccupation with agricultural production, I agree completely with the Director-General of that organization, Dr. B. R. Sen, in his characterization of the next thirty-five years as being the most critical

11 William Letwin, "Four Fallacies About Economic Development," Daedalus, Summer, 1963, quoted in Novack and Lekachman, *Development and Society* (New York: St. Martin's Press, 1964), p. 36.

period in human history. Am I being too unjust when I say that the American people have not properly grasped the issues at stake or even the nature of the problem and for this some at least of the more influential economists must assume some measure of responsibility?

So, to return to my theme—the relevancy of development economics to development—I venture to suggest that much of what is being taught and written in this field is not concerned with the proper goals or the proper measurements of success and is based on a faulty diagnosis of the nature of the problem. Naturally, if the goals and diagnosis are inadequate, the strategy indicated must likewise be. The type of programming with which to implement the strategy must likewise be irrelevant to the real problem of development. Finally, I would suggest that the base of our study must be broadened to include related disciplines. In those universities where increasing emphasis in economics is given to methodology and quantitative, non-normative themes, perhaps the only solution would be the creation of new graduate departments or faculties of development policy, made up of an interdisciplinary group of economists of different specialties, and sociologists, political scientists, economic historians, economic geographers, urban planners and others in recognition of the obvious fact that development is an interdisciplinary problem of which the conventional organizations of universities do not permit adequate treatment, especially in view of recent trends in economics.

In the naming of such departments, I would expressly include the word "policy" since, in this field, a non-normative approach is especially sterile. In fact I cannot conceive of a meaningful treatment of development divorced from norms or values. If this is so, it is infinitely preferable that such norms and values be made explicit and be subject to searching examination, and not be illusive creatures of unknown origins whose very existence is even often denied.

In my view, there is little opportunity to use effectively in the field of development the great advances or refinements in methodology and measurement. Not only are the available statistical data for the most part completely unreliable, but we have not as yet secured any agreement on such basic prerequisites as the nature of the problem, the diagnosis, the goals of policy and the strategy to achieve the goals. Methodology, on which major stress is now laid, comes at the end of these prerequisites as providing aids in the choice of tactics to carry out the selected strategy. If a student's formal course training is limited to two years of graduate study and he expects to work on development problems, he is, I am afraid, in danger of finding that he has acquired a lot of mental luggage of dubious utility while he has not been expected to think very deeply on questions basic to an effective attack on the problems of development. It is not really an answer to say that you are giving him his analytical tools, and that his thinking can come later. If he has not been made aware of the basic issues in his university training, he may well pass through life unaware of their very existence. Two years is a short period, and there is no escape from the necessity of establishing priorities in determining a curriculum. If the priority is to be methodology of a peculiar mathematical type, or theory of a very abstract, symbolic nature, inevitably little time or interest can be accorded a number of most difficult issues in the field of development policy. What I think is indicated is some hard thinking and even soul searching on the nature of your own values in this field.

If, after or even without such soul searching, you decide that economics is to be a non-normative discipline with emphasis on methodology and measurement, as, of course, you have a perfect right to do, then we are still confronted with the question of where and in what subjects should training be offered to students interested in development policy—the subject of life and death concern to two-thirds of the world's population. The only point I am trying to make is that you cannot have it both ways.

I posed this same question at a small informal gathering of economists recently. A distinguished economist retorted that I was asking them to teach people to be wise and that that just could not be done. I do not think that was quite a fair statement of the problem I was raising. It is surely possible to think more or less profoundly (or more or less superficially) even on messy social problems—to subject current and often unchallenged views to critical examination, to probe into the implicit values of a writer, to follow through the implications and probable consequences of various recommended courses of actions. You may not be able to teach a fool to be wise, but surely a function of a university is to aid intelligent people in their pursuit of wisdom. In fact, over one of the gates of Harvard Yard I remember an inscription "Enter and grow in wisdow." Should we change this to read "Enter, and learn methodology?" While methodology may be useful it hardly takes the place of wisdom, and wisdom is what we badly need in this field.

It is again a familiar question of establishing priorities. Personally, in a graduate department of development policy and in the limited time available, I would place emphasis on the ethical problems of values, on the use of basic tools of economic analysis in studying the functioning of economies, and the consequences, actual and probable, of a multitude of policies, on the use of relatively simple statistical methodology, and on the interaction of economic, political and cultural elements in the various main groups of developing societies. Even this may be too heavy a program for two years and certainly does not leave room for many of the methodological courses being offered today. This basic course would be suitable for students intending to specialize in the sociology and political science of underdeveloped societies as well as economic students intending to specialize in planning and policy formulation and in more advanced quantitative methodology. It would, in other words, not restrict our field to a certain type of mind with a certain narrow type of training but would recognize that development is a broad and difficult subject calling for many different types of minds and different kinds of specialities. We have only to contrast this approach with the requirements for the Ph.D. in economics at leading American universities to see the vast difference in point of view and emphasis I am proposing.

IV

Development and the Decline of Competition

In my own thinking I have come to lay increasing stress on imperfect competition as an obstacle to development. It is curious that I came to this so late, as in a memorandum of 1938 I laid much stress on this factor in accounting for the slowness of the recovery movement of that time. On the other hand, it is completely absent from the Mission Report I directed for the World Bank in 1949-50. The explanation, I think, lay in my failure to appreciate until 1960 that the problem of underdevelopment is also a problem of persistent, chronic and massive unemployment. A recognition of this automatically alerts one to the causes of unemployment.

Although there has been much discussion of the problem of combining full employment with stability in recent years, the subject is sufficiently new that the appropriate vocabulary has not as yet been standardized. Paul Samuelson made a valiant attempt to replace the older terms "wage inflation" and "cost push" inflation by the phrase "sellers' inflation" but this does not seem to have caught on. The safest course is still to talk of administered prices and negotiated wages, but this is a clumsy circumlocution. In the policy field, the situation is even worse, with usage ranging from the English phrase "incomes policy" to the awkward American phrase "President Johnson's guidelines of wage and price policy."

Conceptually, we are in much better shape. It has long been a commonplace of economic theory that a price of a good or service may be "too high" in the sense of not permitting the sale of all of an existing stock, or absorption of existing capacity to produce that particular good or service. It is perhaps less obvious, but it has been generally accepted by professional economists, that, *at a given level of national income and monetary demand,* the price of labor may be too high to insure its full employment.[1] This situation may not be subject to correction by a generalized reduction in wages, because of the causal and chain reaction effect leading to successive reductions in aggregate demand, as happened in 1929-33.

As I mentioned earlier, the first term to describe too high wages in this particular sense of the term was "wage inflation," doubtless because wages are obviously an element in the cost of production and the cost of production can equally obviously be too high at a given level of demand. The virtue of Samuelson's phrase "sellers' inflation" is that it permits us to see that the same phenomenon may arise from "too high" profits, which are often not thought of as an element in cost, but rather as the residual between cost and prices. In other words, we can also say that, at a given level of demand, prices may be deliberately "set" too high to absorb productive capacity and insure full employment.

Recently I came across an account of the development by the General Electric Co. of something called a silicone controlled rectifier, which has a multitude of uses for our age of gadgets. It was introduced in 1957 at a cost of three hundred dollars each.

[1] One of the best theoretical expositions with which I am familiar is that of Fritz Machlup in *Essays on Economic Semantics,* Prentice-Hall, Englewood Cliffs, N. J., 1963, pp. 241-268.

It is now being produced at thirty-five cents a unit and General Electric expects to sell 150 million units by 1970. You can imagine what the market would be if the price had remained at three hundred dollars. Whether this is a case of enlightened self-interest or heading off of potential competition, I do not know. But this is how our economic system is ideally supposed to operate and too often, unfortunately, does not.

We may pause for a moment to examine our assumption of a given level of income and demand. Do not the rises in wages and prices of the type under consideration themselves give rise to increases in incomes, demand, production and employment? Barbara Ward cites the case of the early wage rises granted by Henry Ford as being the dynamic factor which created customers for his cars. I think the answer to her point is that it was not the higher incomes of his few workers but the lower prices of his cars that brought about an increase in effective demand and permitted him to pay the higher wages. In other words, if the per unit costs and prices of cars had not declined with the advance in wages, demand would not have increased and with it employment. In this case the higher wages would have been at the expense of profits and we would have had a transfer of buying power rather than an increase. Academic opinion has on balance been opposed to the view expressed by Barbara Ward and frequently by businessmen and trade unions.

Thus Lowell E. Gallaway, dealing only with open unemployment, concludes, after a skillful handling of empirical data, that "the relative price of labor in general has been increased by the actions of labor unions to a level that generates widespread unemployment."[2] He found that wages in strongly organized industries rose relative to unorganized labor. Ranis and Fei,[3] in an article I do not completely understand, prove to their satisfaction that under certain assumptions and with equations of increasing complexity there may never be sufficient mobility to clear up

2 Lowell E. Gallaway, "Labor Mobility, Resource Allocation and Structural Unemployment," A. E. R., 1963, p. 715.
3 Ranis and Fei, *American Economic Review*, Sept. 1961, p. 533.

rural unemployment. Lloyd Reynolds,[4] discussing the continued high level of unemployment in Puerto Rico, is inclined to place major emphasis on too rapid a rise in legal minimum wage rates.

On the other hand John D. Kendrich and Rynzo Sato[5] emphasize the role of rising wage rates in bringing about a shift in purchasing power from capital owners as a class to labor as a class, thus maintaining markets and employment. (I suppose others would prefer to say that this process decreases the propensity to save.) While I think this is a defensible point of view for an advanced stage of industrialization, by dealing with aggregates it tends to obscure what may be happening to the allocation of labor within the group. Moreover, if less saving is advisable, it may be brought about in other and more socially desirable ways, for example, by the provision of services by public bodies.

Alvin Hansen[6] has little patience with cautious formulations, and plunges into the matter with his customary gusto and comes up with a rather diabolical suggestion: "but is it not sheer madness to continue the obsolete fiction that the public has no stake in collective bargining in a society so highly interdependent as ours? If no agreement can be reached, the government should recommend a settlement. The facts about wages, costs and profits should be made public. No corporation should be allowed to raise prices for a period of, say, six months after the agreement has been put into effect." He continues "Now that the government offers management and labor the protective canopy of full employment policies, powerful trade unions and giant corporations can scarcely claim the right to raise wages and prices in the dark."

Clearly, the weight of academic opinion not only as a matter of static theory but in a moving dynamic situation, is that imperfect competition, both in industry and in the labor market,

[4] Lloyd Reynolds, *Wages and Employment in a Labor Surplus Economy*, A. E. R., March 1965, pp. 19-39.

[5] John D. Kendrich and Rynzo Sato, *Factor Prices, Productivity and Economic Growth*, A. E. R., 1963, p. 975.

[6] Alvin Hansen, *Economic Issues of the 60s* (Cambridge: Harvard University Press, 1960), pp. 37-38.

is a contributing factor to persistent unemployment which may not be subject to correction by increasing aggregate money demand, and may even force monetary inflation to maintain an existing level of employment. On the other hand, a decline in general wage rates because of its cumulative, causative effect may not stimulate employment, but that case is hardly an issue today.

What has all this to do with development? Much more, I think, than with the problems of growth, full employment and stability in developed countries, where it has received almost all the attention from academic writers. Let me defend this perhaps surprising statement.

Most of the really decisive steps in the development of what are now called developed countries took place in the nineteenth and first few decades of the present century when competition and freely moving prices were reasonably effective in securing the requisite movement of people from farm to non-farm activities and in bringing about the rise in economic and educational levels necessary to bring about a marked decline in birth and population growth rates. The tremendous growth in employment in the 1940's, fifties and sixties has been entirely in the multitude of service industries where the economies of scale are not so obvious and where a considerable degree of competition, both in prices and as between workers, still prevails. All these factors have maintained a reasonably effective mobility of labor and a tendency, except in specific pockets, for wage rates to tend toward equality almost regardless of the nature of the work. Thus the reallocation of factors necessitated by the astonishing spurt in physical productivity in agriculture and in industrial production, suggested by economic theory, is more or less taking place, not without friction, support prices and individual suffering, but nevertheless, in the perspective of a decade, the machinery of allocating resources in developed countries is still functioning reasonably well, particularly as applied to the distribution of the annual crop of new workers.

As R. J. Ball remarks "There is considerable evidence of a strong tendency for the level of wages to rise uniformly over all industries in developed countries since the Second World War, little affected by relative differences in economic conditions prevailing between industries."[7] Note that he restricts this generalization to developed countries. Where it is not functioning properly, it seems to me, is in the underdeveloped countries, either in securing a proper mix of factors, or in the type of goods and services actually produced. Let me take up the first point first.

My old teacher, Jacob Viner, for whom I have a great respect and affection, once said that there was nothing treated by the concept of disguised unemployment that could not just as well or better be treated by the concept of productivity of the employed approaching zero.[8] In this I must disagree largely on the grounds of semantics. The remedy for unemployment that immediately comes to mind is employment, while the remedy for low productivity is likely to be a host of things to increase productivity. Since productivity as applied to a group is converted to value terms and becomes indistinguishable from income, we get tangled up in the tautological mess of making income depend on income. Or if we try to stick to productivity in a physical sense, we may end up by advocating action to increase agricultural production as a whole, thus decreasing still further incomes or productivity in a value sense. We avoid these dangerous pitfalls by thinking of the poorest class of farmers as being unemployed, in the sense that the sum total of production would be affected very little if they all suddenly disappeared or stopped work altogether.

Another way of looking at this would be to say that if the gap between urban and organized workers' pay and that of the rural and unorganized workers' remuneration is steadily widening, something serious has happened to the machinery of the mobility of labor, and labor is being very badly allocated. If, in addition, to improve agricultural "productivity," large sums are diverted by

[7] R. J. Ball, *Inflation and the Theory of Money* (London: George Allen and Unwin, 1964), p. 139.
[8] Jacob Viner, *The Indian Journal of Economics*, July, 1957, p. 23.

public agencies to agriculture, there is a further malallocation of resources. The test of sufficiency in mobility, or goodness or badness in allocation of resources, can only be whether inequality of income is being increased or decreased. The proof, then, of the inadequacy of mobility is the inequality existing in incomes from work.

There has been little empirical work done on this problem. Albert Berry of Yale, in an as yet un-published work, presented data for Colombia tending to show that real agricultural wages had not risen for nearly thirty-eight years up to 1963, which would suggest that the incomes of the agricultural self-employed actually declined. For urban industrial workers, from 1955 to 1962, real wages and fringe benefits rose by the astonishing amount of sixty-five percent.

In my study of the cotton industry in Colombia real wages of three big textile companies consuming eighty-five percent of the cotton from 1957 to 1962 rose by forty percent while per capita real income in the country as a whole apparently rose by something less than one percent a year.[9] Carl Shoup,[10] for Venezuela, estimated that the bottom forty-three percent of the population earned only ten percent of the national income in 1957. Milton Taylor, et al.,[11] for Colombia for 1961, estimated that the top two percent of the population received twenty percent of the income whereas the bottom twenty-five percent received five percent. Charles Kindleberger gathered together scattered data for various countries tending to confirm this gross inequality, suggesting that the top ten percent receive from thirty-five to forty-five percent of the income and that the lower the per capita income, the greater the degree of inequality.[12]

[9] Lauchlin Currie, *El Algodón en Colombia* (Bogotá: Foundation for the Progress of Colombia, 1963), p. 83.
[10] Carl Shoup et al., *The Fiscal System of Venezuela* (Baltimore: The Johns Hopkins Press, 1965), p. 24.
[11] Milton Taylor et al., *The Fiscal System of Colombia* (Baltimore: The Johns Hopkins Press, 1965), p. 2.
[12] Charles Kindleberger, *Economic Development* (New York: McGraw-Hill Co., 1958), p. 8.

I have found, in teaching, that students find it difficult to distinguish between the effects of inequality of income and cost-push or sellers' inflation. This is not surprising since both affect the allocation of resources. The difference, however, is that inequality is not incompatible with full employment—the classic example was pyramid building in Egypt—whereas a growth in inequality in wage or profit rates associated with a rise in prices (or a failure of prices to fall with growing efficiency of production) may dampen down effective demand, production, industrial employment and the efficient functioning of the resource-allocation mechanism. Sellers' inflation is a dynamic process and is treated in relation to costs, prices and demand (as in our silicone rectifier example) whereas existing inequality or growing inequality unassociated with costs and prices may not affect employment but rather change its composition.

What I have tried to suggest up to this point is that typically underdeveloped countries possess an army of economically unemployed far exceeding the proportion of the working force recorded as unemployed in the depths of the Great Depression in developed countries; that they are characterized, as one might expect from this fact, by great inequality of income and that this inequality is probably growing. To this picture let us now add two more elements: an industry characterized in large part by imperfect competition and economies characterized by rapidly growing populations and working forces.

I do not think that I need labor these points. The combination of relatively small markets, economies of scale and modern technology tends on balance to make for relatively few industrial units in many fields and consequently for a lessening in competition in at least prices. Underdeveloped countries tend to keep their silicone rectifiers at three hundred dollars apiece. Similarly the great advances in medicine and the existence of large masses of rural people living on a subsistence basis form the bases of the demographic explosion.

Putting these pieces of the jigsaw puzzle together, a rather alarming picture emerges. The economic mechanism in many or most underdeveloped countries, looked at unemotionally and rationally, is functioning badly. The demographic explosion and the technical revolution in agriculture ought rationally to call for a massive reallocation of the labor force from rural to urban regions and from farming to non-farming occupations. The reallocation that is taking place is in reality not sufficient to provide truly remunerative jobs for the increase in the working force, to say nothing of decent jobs for a large proportion of the existing labor force. It is not that the people do not have unsatisfied needs but rather that the economic system is not organized to permit them to satisfy these needs. At the same time the machine, operating obediently in response to a distorted pattern of demand, is diverting resources to the production of luxury homes, the purchase and assembly of cars, foreign travel, synthetic fibre plants, an enormous quantity of personal services and so on. We are presented with the same tragic absurdity we were presented with in the United States in the 1930's and which we had thought that we had completely outgrown.

True, the causes of the breakdown of the resources allocation mechanism are different. In the 1930's in the United States we were caught in a vicious circle of falling aggregate demand, price and wage rigidities, excess capacity, reduced investment, falling demand. It took us an incredible time and a lot of improvisation before we were able to diagnose the trouble. In fact, it was the combination of war and price controls that finally provided sufficient aggregate demand on the one hand and restraint on sellers' inflation on the other to enable us to operate our productive plant at full capacity.

In the underdeveloped world of today the failure lies not in inadequate growth in aggregate money demand but rather in effective demand, and an essential element in this inadequacy must be sought in the chronic rise of industrial wages, profits and prices above the national gains in production per capita. We have the medical anomaly of suffering from hardening of the arteries at a young and tender age, industrially speaking. The obvious solution of the problem, as throughout the thirties, is to increase aggregate effective demand, production, employment, saving-investment, demand again and so forth. But the conventional first step in the beneficent chain reaction is an increase in money demand. If this is promptly offset by a corresponding or more than corresponding rise in industrial prices and incomes, the first step is abortive and becomes the last step, and the beneficent circle cannot get underway. The take-off does not take place and instead we witness only a painful crawl.

It may be objected that while the point is theoretically valid, the small degree of industrialization and unionization robs it of much of its practical importance. True, these may be an impediment to industrialization but there are some six or seven urban workers to each worker in industry so there is still ample scope for the play of competition and mobility.

This objection overlooks the fact that, given more or less uniform urban wages, there is a certain relation between the number of workers engaged in the making of goods and those employed in distributing and maintaining them, in constructing buildings and providing services. If this relation changes in response to wide variations in wages the allocation of resources becomes less economic, mechanization may be excessive in the high wage industry and deficient in the low wage fields and labor is in effect wasted or underemployed.

In a highly developed economy, like the United States, the great growth in demand, and consequently employment, has been in service industries where competition, both as between companies and among workers, has had much fuller sway. The need in underdeveloped countries is still weighted on the side of goods rather than services (with the important exception of services provided by public entities such as teachers, hospitals and so forth). One cannot look with complacency upon a decline in industrial employment in underdeveloped countries as in developed economies if it arises not from a voluntary shift of consumption on the part of a relatively egalitarian society but from inequality and insufficient effective demand for what people badly need.

In short, in a "pain" economy, we would normally look to the mass consumption industries as being the most dynamic and rapidly growing sector, leading to a six to seven fold growth in complementary urban occupations. To dampen down the growth of what should be the most rapidly growing sector is to dampen down the growth of all.

True, it is not quite as simple as this. The malallocation of resources in the public sector, growing inequality, monetary inflation, ill conceived improvisations, loss of confidence, flight of capital and the horrible dead weight of a three percent annual growth in population all play their role. But many of these things were true in what we now call developed countries in the nineteenth century. One principal difference was that the resource allocation mechanism of competition and mobility was sufficiently efficient in the earlier period to permit a breaking of the vicious circle of poverty-high birth rate-poverty without conscious state intervention or planning.

In most of the underdeveloped world this does not take place, and with every day that passes the problems become more acute and, because of the population explosion, greater in magnitude. The economic organization is not giving, or I should say is not being permitted to give, adequate employment and production, and certainly is not providing a defensible distribution.

The desperate seriousness of the Colombian situation, for example, is indicated by a study of the Mexican case. Despite an excellent balance of payments and the appearance of substantial progress in a few cities, Raymond Vernon concludes that "the urban poor, the ejidal farmers and the small landowners—making up perhaps two/thirds or three/quarters of the country—may have to be regarded as simply outside the market for many modern day products."[13] And as a consequence, I might add, the population continues to grow at more than a three percent annual rate. As in Mexico, so in Colombia the real problem is excessive parcelization, not great estates, and rural poverty and

13 Raymond Vernon, *The Dilemma of Mexico's Development* (Cambridge: Harvard University Press, 1963), p. 184.

not inadequate agricultural production. The big difference can be found in the balance of payments.

The solution follows, or at least should follow, from the diagnosis. The vicious circle that prevents the take-off must somehow, in some way, be broken. For this reason I call for a breakthrough plan in my book on the acceleration of development. This suggests the necessity and the means of achieving a deliberate and massive concentration of effort to raise within a decade the economic, educational and cultural level of the poorest half or more of the population. I would not for a moment minimize the magnitude of the effort required. On the other hand, I would equally insist on the tremendous and continuing returns that would follow a successful effort. Moreover, the cost in terms of foreign assistance and the internal effort required would probably be much less than the indefinite continuance of the present desultory and pointless policy of lending and refinancing which supplies just enough to keep up a modicum of services for a continually expanding population, but not enough to check that expansion.

However, I have become convinced that the breakthrough requires, as an indispensable condition, what the British call "an incomes policy" in important segments of the economy, especially in the industrial sector where groups in a strong bargaining position have become entrenched. This seems to me to be an infinitely more important and urgent necessity in underdeveloped than in developed countries and also, I might add, a much more difficult policy for which to secure acceptance and execution.

Up to now, in, I believe, all Latin American countries, the governing class has made its peace with organized labor by securing and sharing a larger portion of a slowly growing production. This has been done not only in negotiated wage agreements and advances in prices but also in the numerous fringe benefits provided by such agreements and by the "advanced" labor legislation. All this in reality, though I am sure unconsciously, has been at the expense of the unorganized and self-employed and, equally important, at the expense of a vigorous and dynamic growth in the production of articles of mass consumption. (So little is the economic process understood that virtually all regard the gains of organized labor as signifying gains for the whole economy.) How can we change this ingrained mentality and remove one of the chief barriers to industrialization and development? In the field of policy, it is obvious that we are here confronted with a problem of the utmost difficulty. Even in the United States, large groups even up until today were able to obtain very little share in the growing income. Transpose the problem to underdeveloped countries, where (a) tax enforcement is weak and tax exemptions abound, (b) competition in industry is very imperfect indeed, (c) labor unions and labor codes are strong and (d) over half the working force is unemployed and lives on the margin of subsistence, (e) inflation is chronic, and (f) there is complete inability to distinguish demagoguery from reform—where, I repeat, these are the conditions, the distribution of income becomes a highly arbitrary and even capricious operation. If there is any rule of the game, it comes dangerously close to the Biblical pronouncement quoted by Myrdal "For unto every one that hath shall be given, and he shall have abundance; but from him that hath not shall be taken away even that which he hath."[14]

Please do not misunderstand me. I am not raising a battlecry. I am merely, as an economist, stating a situation and a problem. All that economic theory can tell us is that enough must be paid for any service to call forth the requisite marginal supply to satisfy the marginal demand at the price people are prepared to pay. But in the absence of mobility and competition, this rule is consistent with very wide and ethically indefensible variations in incomes.

Assuming an incomes policy is a necessary component of a Breakthrough Plan for underdeveloped countries, how does one go about getting its acceptance? The economic sophistication— I don't even mention patriotism—required of the presently privileged groups (and for the present purpose I include trade union leaders and members in such groups) appals me. Even a Labor Government in England has not been able to keep its trade union

14 St. Matthew XXV: 29.

members in line and is having to resort to the old measures of overall restraint on aggregate money demand. For five years I have been warning and exhorting my fellow Colombians with a notable lack of success. Sometimes I remind myself of the little man in the advertisements of the *Philadelphia Bulletin* frantically and vainly trying to call the attention of an indifferent audience to an urgent danger or strange phenomenon.

Rather in desperation, I have come to look to the American and international lending agencies to lead the way to a new Marshall Plan and lay down the requisite conditions for such a plan, but I know that before that can happen the economists of the leading universities must first be convinced of the necessity. This, I am afraid, is going to take time, and time, again I am afraid, is what we lack. Vicious circles and geometrical progression in population growth form a dangerous combination. While we are debating whether a change in the rules of the game is or is not necessary, and if so, what changes are necessary, other "practical" people are probing around the poor economic mechanism—poking buttons here, pulling levers there, smashing gauges if they register danger signs, poking screwdrivers into delicate parts and even occasionally hitting the thing with a hammer. Quite oblivious of the corpus of economics, we encourage monopoly on the one hand and impose price control in the remaining competitive areas. The next step, of course, will probably be the triumphant demonstration that the system does not work and has to be scrapped and replaced. Meanwhile population grows inexorably.

In a problem of this nature a major job of education and persuasion is indispensable. Industrialists and trade union leaders must become convinced that their true interests are bound up with the wider interests of the society. They must become convinced that, as part of a carefully thought out and financed overall national job creation plan designed to eliminate the worst features of poverty, they have everything to gain and nothing to lose. I regret to have to say that I doubt whether their own political leaders wish to or can carry this conviction. Only as part of a treaty-like international Marshall Plan which has had a success-ful tryout in some suitable country with abundant study and ex-planation, can one hope to persuade the industrialists and union leaders and rank and file where their true interests lie.

It can be seen how far a deeper probing of the problem of underdevelopment takes us from the Well Intentioned Sprinkler Approach or the Fundamental Equation of Growth Approach that are currently in vogue.

V

*Population and Development**

There has been, in the past few years, a tremendous discussion of the population problem and what should be done about it. There has been surprisingly little attempt, however, to define the nature of the problem or, perhaps I should say, distinguish between the different aspects of the problem. This is perhaps because it is a multi-disciplinary matter, and the various disciplines have been naturally interested only in those aspects that immediately concern them. Among those who have written and talked about the problem are the agricultural economists, the agronomists and food scientists generally, the demographers, the sociologists, the economists, the medical profession, conservationists, city planners, social workers, the clergy and many others. As in so many human problems, one is continually reminded of the blind man describing that part of the elephant he has happened to touch. It is, in other words, extraordinarily difficult to see the elephant as a whole or, to drop the metaphor, to grasp the problem as a whole or in its most important aspects.

In this lecture I shall emphasize the economic aspects not only,

* This lecture was originally delivered to the Annual Meeting of the Phi Beta Kappa Society at M.S.U. A revised version was published by the Population Reference Bureau.

I hope, because I happen to be an economist, but also because I believe the economic aspects to be the most basic from the point of view of human well-being.

Let me begin with a few perhaps obvious but nevertheless extremely important statements. Man, in common with all forms of life, has been endowed with a tremendous capacity to reproduce his kind. The interplay of evolutionary forces and ecological balance has provided those forms of life that have persisted with a sufficiently prodigal capacity and desire to reproduce their kind as to insure their continuance. Given this capacity, as the environment changes so the actual extent of reproduction changes. Environmental changes in the past century or so have altered enormously in favor of the survival of man. However, his sexual nature and his capacity to reproduce have not altered in the slightest. Hence the demographic explosion.

Philip Hauser has illustrated the magnitude of this explosion in dramatic terms. Of his many calculations I will cite only a few. "It is estimated that for the some 600,000 years of the Paleolithic Age (the old Stone Age) population growth perhaps approximated 0.02 per thousand per year. . . . The rate of world population growth continued to accelerate after World War II, so that in 1965 it approximated twenty per thousand per year. . . . In the course of man's inhabitation of this globe, then, his rate of population growth has increased from a rate of about 2 percent *per millennium* to 2 percent *per year,* a thousandfold increase in growth rate.[1] . . . During the second half of this century, there will be a greater increase in world population than was achieved in all the millennia of human existence up to the present time."[2]

The causes of the upsetting of the human ecological balance, of course, can be found in advances in science and technology which have made possible both an astounding increase in food production and a decline in the death rate and a lengthening of the longevity of man, while fertility rates have remained high;

[1] Philip Hauser, "Population, Poverty and World Politics," *University of Illinois Bulletin,* Urbana, Illinois, Vol. 62, No. 97, June, 1965, p. 3.
[2] *Ibid.,* p. 7.

probably little below those of the Stone Age. The application of technology and the consequences of this application have by no means run their course. "Between 1940 and 1960 Mexico, Costa Rica, Venezuela, Ceylon, Malaya and Singapore decreased their death rate by more than 50 percent in less than a decade."[3] There are still great possibilities of reducing the infantile death rate in all rural and underdeveloped countries, where most of the world's population lives, and of growing more food to support more people.

In the case of Latin America, if the rate of population continues unchecked, the population will triple from 1960 to the year 2000, or will grow from 200 million to 650 million. In Colombia, the population is doubling every twenty-two years or so. That is, without a rapid and appreciable fall in the birth rate, Colombia could have a population of some seventy million in forty-five years.

As Professor Hauser says "the present rate of world population growth cannot possibly persist for very long. As a matter of fact . . . any rate of population growth would in time saturate the globe and exhaust space itself."[4] The only question is whether the inevitable decline in the rate of growth and the achievement of some equilibrium will come about through a renewed great increase in the death rate, signifying misery and suffering on an unprecedented scale, or a drastic fall in the birth rate. Over the longer run, *there are no other solutions.* The increase in numbers in all other forms of life is checked by death. To man only is granted the chance to achieve a balance through a decline in the rate of reproduction.

But I am getting ahead of my story. I must first show why the problem is not one for the long run—of space or of food—but is urgent, immediate and actual. This is supremely important since usually man is not distinguished by his foresight or concern for the long run. He is generally aroused only when the actual crisis is upon him. My argument is that the crisis is actually upon us

3 *Ibid.,* p. 7.
4 *Ibid.,* p. 5.

here and now, that it is already late and that the principal
barrier to development, with all that this implies, can be found in
the excessive rate of population growth.

Let me first try to clear up some misconceptions. The essence of
a state of development, it appears to me, is not merely a question
of keeping alive under any conditions. It is, rather, the possession
of widely diffused and rising cultural, educational and economic
levels, a sense of improvement and betterment, and a widespread
conviction in the justice and efficiency of the economic and political systems under which one is living—in short, a sense of dominance or purposeful control over one's environment. This cannot
be obtained by merely keeping people from starving. It implies,
among other things, a growing abundance of goods and services,
good health services, educational opportunities, decent housing,
diversions, leisure and a sense of advancement in one's work.
Under such conditions life can become more gracious, social
conflicts can become less sharp, and more attention can be paid
to what J. K. Galbraith has aptly called the quality of living.

Can this state be obtained with a doubling of the population
every twenty or thirty years? Perhaps for a short time and under
exceptionally favorable circumstances, but certainly not in most
underdeveloped countries today. The reason is really very simple.
A compound rate of growth in population of, say, three percent
per annum means an unfavorable relation of workers to dependents with over half the population being under eighteen
years of age; it means that most of the saving and investment
must be devoted to supplying the needs of the additional people,
rather than to raising the standards of the existing number;
it means resorting to less favorable and less accessible land; it
means the assignment of large sums to the infrastructure of
transport and services rather than to a more immediate raising
of the standard of living of the poor; it means the destruction of
natural resources of forests, fish, top soils and the more rapid
using up of irreplaceable resources of energy; and it means the
continuance of woefully inadequate educational opportunities.
All this, in turn, spells continued poverty, frustration, hate and

envy, inability to cope with problems that grow in magnitude with every passing day, a lessening faith in the justice and efficiency of both the systems of free private enterprise and democracy, and, naturally, diffusion of efforts, improvisation and demagogy with their inevitable results. In short, a rapid growth in population in underdeveloped areas today prevents them from utilizing technology to achieve an assured dominance or control over their social, economic, cultural or political environment.

If this does not constitute a crisis, I do not know what the word means. At the present rate of growth, for example, the population of Bogotá, Colombia, would grow from two million to eight million in twenty-two years. One can imagine the resources that would have to be devoted to the public services and to the moving of the additional people and the goods they require to maintain merely the existing standards. It is estimated that the population of Bogotá will increase from 2 million in 1967 to 3.6 million in 1976. To provide public services, roads and housing adequately for the growth in this single city would require sums very large in relation to the current national budget or even the volume of national savings. These necessary expenditures, it may be noted, are to look after only some of the needs of new inhabitants and are not to raise the level of living of existing inhabitants. And they in no sense represent permanent solutions of an ever-growing problem. We are now proposing to devote more of our scanty savings to the growing of more agricultural goods for domestic consumption. But true development should correspond with a smaller proportion of our resources being devoted to agriculture. England, for example, supplies over seventy percent of its food and wool with some four percent of its annual investment. I am not saying that we should not spend more; I am merely saying that it is a pity that we have to, assuming we do.

You can, I hope, now see that growing more food is not the solution of underdevelopment; it is a painful and regrettable necessity forced on us by the rapid growth in population and the failure to achieve development in the true sense of the term. If we arrive at the point where fifty percent of the working force in underdeveloped countries not only is nominally engaged, as at present, but actually is needed to grow food efficiently for the other fifty percent, we will have already lost the battle for development and be where India is today. You can also understand why economists cannot get excited over the possibilities of keeping more billions of people alive from proteins from the sea or from a yeast made from petroleum, prospects announced by technicians in other fields. Apparently we must repeat again and again that man does not live by bread alone.

But, some of you may object, is it not a fact that a rapid growth in population creates new demands and "is good for business," and hence for development? Such a view, I am afraid, only illustrates a confusion of needs with effective demand. The fallacy may be seen by comparing the small effective demand of the nearly five hundred million Indians with the relatively large effective demand of the twenty million Canadians. To add to the number of very poor country people creates little additional buying power. A stationary population does not mean a stationary effective demand. On the contrary, as a general rule, the more slowly a population is increasing, the more rapid is the growth in income per capita and gross income and hence buying power in absolute terms. The end of development is not a growing demand for the bare elements of life, but a demand that proceeds from a high and rising income for all the things other than food.

Another type of argument is based on a logical fallacy. Since Mexico and Venezuela in recent years experienced both the highest rate of growth in gross product and in population, it is suggested that the former must in some way be due to the latter. This is known as the fallacy of *post hoc ergo propter hoc*. It reminds me of the ingenious sunspot theory of trade cycles, based on a presumed correlation of cycles of sunspots and of trade. Apart from the fact that the correlation was faulty, no satisfactory causal connection could be established. It is not difficult to establish that the high rates of growth in the gross product of both Mexico and Venezuela arose from other circumstances, and that the extraordinarily high proportion of children in the population added nothing to production, imposed a drag on savings and a serious threat for the future. Similarly, one would have difficulty in establishing a causal connection between the slower rate of growth in the gross product in Argentina and its lower rate of population growth. Many excellent explanations of Argentina's difficulties have been written but none, so far as I know, place the blame on the relatively lower rate of population growth.

Let me turn now to a more difficult point. Since it obviously would be useless to advocate family planning to an individual family on the grounds of helping the development of the country, the arguments used are always the health of the mother and the ability to provide a decent living and education for the children. While understandable and indeed unavoidable, reliance on this argument has several weaknesses. It implies, for example, that if a family is in comfortable circumstances there is no reason why it should not have a relatively large number of children.

It is generally thought that the size of a family is solely the concern of the individual parents and that the state has no concern in the matter. Even the arguments of the advocates of family planning implicitly concede this point. But is it true? If the problem is properly stated and understood in its social, economic and political significance the society and hence its collective organization, the state, has a vital interest and responsibility. If all couples decide to have ten children, the consequence for the society would be catastrophic in a very short time. With a lowering of the standard of living of the many, in a world in which the expenditures of the few are rising spectacularly and conspicuously, the destructive emotions of envy, jealousy and hate flourish; religion and morality decline; and the prestige of the economic and political systems fall even though the root cause may be found in the excessive rate of growth in population.

If, I repeat, the problem is properly grasped in all its ramifications, the interests of the community and the state lie in preventing this excessive growth. In this matter the interest of the individual must be subordinated to that of the community. We must in every way try to accelerate the process of adjustment of our thinking and attitudes to the changed realities of today and reduce the inevitable misery and suffering that result from every day's delay in gaining some measure of conscious control over our environment. What all this adds up to is that we, collectively, are not exercising any purposeful control of our environment. One of the principal elements in this loss of control can be found in the unrestrained growth in population. Is this not a concern of all of us, and of the only organization through which we can effectively express our collective will, the state?

Let me return for a moment to the argument that it is all right for people who can afford to to have larger families. But surely higher birth rates and rates of population growths, from whatever class, increase the ratio of people to capital and resources. Indeed, the children of the wealthy make much more drain on the resources of the community than those of the poor, precisely because their standards of consumption and of education are so much higher. When they are of marriageable age, each child expects a costly house, car and so on. To an economist, the fact that they can pay for this additional consumption is irrelevant. From the point of view of the real income of the society—the volume of consumers goods and services annually produced—increased consumption by the wealthy and their families means less saving by them, less consumption available for the poor, and less future production. The burden of the well-to-do, in real economic terms, is not measured by their income but by their consumption.[5] As for the distribution of wealth argument, there are other ways of doing this without entailing so much consumption.

Sometimes one encounters the argument that it is good for the wealthy to have large families as they can provide them with good education. This is also open to the excessively high consumption objection, in this case to absorbing more of the scanty

---

[5] For what they are worth, the national accounts of Colombia indicate no net "household" saving i.e. individual saving, in recent years. This at least is not inconsistent with the possibility mentioned in the text, though not much reliance can be had on the data.

educational facilities or foreign exchange resources. However, the most effective objection is probably that if there is a need for more highly or at least more expensively educated children, it would be socially better to provide for this through scholarships to poorer children. Proven ability, rather than wealth, should be the criterion for admittance to universities.

Even in a wealthy country like the United States, the birth rate and rate of increase in population can be excessive in terms of the quality of life. In the private-car, suburban-living, vacation-minded civilization of the United States, every person demands an inordinate amount of space and that is just what is lacking even in that vast country. It will not be long, I venture to guess, before even very wealthy states will be actively concerned with the regulation of their numbers and where every additional child in a family of more than two children will be progressively and heavily taxed. Even more drastic measures may have to be taken to check the size of the families of the very poor.

Stephan Enke has developed an ingenious argument for giving bonuses (partly retained in a savings fund until past child bearing age) to women for years of non-births, to be sacrificed if and when births occur.[6] These and other schemes are designed to strengthen the motivation of the practice of family planning. Such payments could be financed in part by steeply progressive taxes on the larger families of the wealthy.

One occasionally encounters another type of argument which runs somewhat as follows: often it appears that very poor people with large families are happier than richer people. This might be the case, for example, in the fishing villages on the Colombian Coast where the work is not too difficult and is interesting and the sun, wind, water and abundant fish protein make for a relatively healthy existence. Who am I to impose my values on them? If they want to live as they are, why not let them?

The answer to these questions, I think, is that, as long as they are residents of the country, the state must impose its values.

6 Stephan Enke, *Economics for Development*, Prentice-Hall, Inc., Englewood Cliffs, N. J., 1963, pp. 377-379.

The fish can be exhausted by the growing population; it is difficult to deny additional health and educational services; the rapidly growing young population will drift to the larger towns and cities and expect work. So here, again, the size of families resulting from a way of life is a matter of national concern. The family planning of urban people is of limited national value if the large rural population continues to have a high birth rate. Sooner or later this high birth rate will make its inexorable demands on the savings and resources of the country and will prejudice the condition of all. We share a national patrimony and are jointly and collectively responsible for it.

This last point brings us to a second weakness of the current argument for family planning. It does not appear to be very effective with the people for whom it is most needed—the very poor and particularly the rural poor. These are the people who one might assume would be most anxious to engage in family planning and doubtless many are. It seems to be the general experience, however, that the poorest and the least educated are the most difficult to reach and influence, even in developed countries. According to Hauser "Efforts to decrease birth rates among the mass populations of the world characterized by illiteracy and poverty have thus far had little success."[7]

In a developed country an authoritative study found from 1890 to 1940 a high inverse relationship between the economic and educational levels (up to the fourth year of high school) and birth rates.[8] This correlation did not appear to be affected by other factors, such as religion.

These weaknesses of the self-interest propaganda for family planning suggest that it would be prudent to lay more stress on the national economic argument to influence both the objectives of national development plans and legislation. If, as weighty evidence suggests, high birth rates form the principal obstacle

7 *Ibid.*, p. 16.
8 Richard and Nancy Ruggles, Demographic and Economic Change in Developed Countries; A conference, National Bureau of Economic Research (Princeton: Princeton University Press, 1960), pp. 155-193.

to development, then the state cannot remain indifferent to such rates and at the same time be concerned with development. It is partly for this reason that I have argued that we should change the development objective in underdeveloped countries from that of a rate of increase in the gross real product per capita to a rapid rise in the economic and educational levels of the poorest half or more of the population. I also argued that the strategy of development indicated was not just to secure *any* reduction in mass poverty but rather a *sufficient* reduction to break the vicious circle of poverty—ignorance—high birth rates—poverty. This may very well require a massive once-and-for-all effort—what I called a Breakthrough and what Leibenstein has called "the critical minimum effort."[9]

This does not for a moment mean that we should relax the family planning effort. Rather it means that both efforts, family planning and economic and social planning, should be coordinated and pushed at the same time. It is possible that we may be on the threshold of technological advances that may make family planning, either voluntary or powerfully influenced, more practicable for the rural poor as well as other groups. But nothing will be lost and much gained by proceeding on the assumption that a rapid rise in the educational and economic status of the poor should be the chief objective of economic policy.

In passing, I would call attention to the inconsistences of encouraging larger families through the system of family allowances and tax exemptions. This probably cannot be touched for existing worker families. It is a grave question, however, whether the benefits should be extended to additional children after a certain date in the future. We must create a consciousness that families of more than two or three, whether the parents are rich or poor or middle-class, intensify the problem of achieving development, a most urgent international objective. This can only come about through a widespread understanding of the economics of development and of the relation of population growth to development. In focusing our sights only on individual family planning for

[9] Harvey Leibenstein, *op. cit.*, Chapter 8.

the poor we run the danger of not grasping the national and international crisis aspect of the problem.

There are those who feel that nothing can be done until certain religious attitudes change. This change is actually occurring with surprising rapidity, but in view of the crisis, with not enough rapidity even as yet. Here again, the nature of the catastrophe on a grand and terrifying scale must be constantly stressed and this brings us back again to the economic and social consequences of the upsetting of the human ecological balance. It is possible that the importance of the religious factor has been somewhat exaggerated. At least in developed countries the size of Catholic families, for example, has not differed markedly from non-Catholic families of the same economic and educational level. In under-developed countries the influence has not been subject to as careful and objective study as it clearly deserves. In some regions, it appears to be important; in others, of minor importance.

For so much of man's history, high fertility was so indispens-able for the perpetuation of a tribe or people that it very naturally acquired re-enforcement and encouragement from religion. This can be clearly seen in the Old Testament and reflects the struggle of the Jews, as a people, for survival. Now that the problem has become completely the reverse it is beginning to be seen that the encouragement of higher standards of morality and ethics is more closely related to family planning than to unrestrained propagation. It is devotedly to be hoped that the full implications of the change in the nature of the problem will be grasped as soon as possible so that the forces of religion may truly further the spiritual and moral welfare of man.

It may be noted that the problem with which we are dealing has nothing whatever to do with the economic or political orga-nization of a state. It confronts equally democratic and non-demo-cratic political systems as well as private enterprise and socialist economic systems. In Hungary, Rumania and Czechoslovakia, population growth has stopped almost completely and Red China has reversed its earlier policy of encouraging unrestricted growth. On the other hand, India as yet has had little success and the situation there is becoming highly critical. Hauser's generalization to the effect that "for the world as a whole, poverty is associated with relatively high rates of population increase"[10] appears sound.

It is to be hoped, therefore, that family planning will not be allowed to be presented as a sinister American plot directed against the underdeveloped countries. The best assurance against acceptance of this charge is that the peoples of underdeveloped countries themselves should take the lead in the movement to save their countries in this matter. In retrospect, perhaps the most serious charge that can be made against the British regime in India is that it did nothing to discourage the unrestrained growth in population. On the other hand, by promoting public medicine and sanitation, it intensified the problem. How complex and difficult life can become!

I should like to add a few more words, stressing once more the overwhelming importance of the economic and the time aspects of the problem. Let me take a recent example from Colombia. From 1951 to 1964 there occurred a veritable technical revolution in agriculture plus the opening of large extensions of rich, alluvial areas in the Magdalena and Sinu Valleys and east and south-east of Villavicencio to the east of Bogotá, all capable of mechanization and all accessible by new means of transport. The population increased by more than fifty percent in this period of thirteen years, of which a major portion was urban, which generally consumes more calories per capita. Despite this notable increase in effective demand, agricultural prices did not rise in relation to other prices. In view of the well known high inelasticity of demand for agricultural goods which results in a large rise in prices when there is a small decrease in supply, the inference seems inescapable that there must have been an increase in production for domestic consumption of over sixty percent in this short period, a truly remarkable performance.

Did the country gain greatly from this technical and transport revolution and the opening of rich new lands? Very little. Country people appear to be, if anything, even poorer than

10 Hauser, p. 10.

they were in 1951, with more tiny farms and squatters. It is questionable whether urban people are consuming much more food per capita. There has been some release, in relative terms, of country people for the production of non-agricultural goods, although in absolute terms the rural population has continued to increase. Part of this gain in non-agricultural production was offset by the worsening in the condition of some country people and by the destruction of natural resources. Most of the remarkable gain in agricultural production went to supply the food requirements of more people.

The seriousness of this may not be immediately apparent. It is that we cannot expect an indefinite repetition of the favorable conditions of the 1950's. Successive increases of fifty or sixty percent in each thirteen years will require higher capital input, recourse to less fertile or less accessible land, and more people in agriculture. If we should reach the stage where forty to fifty percent of the working is actually needed to produce the food for the others we will indeed be in a bad way. But if the population continues to grow at a compound rate of three percent per annum this may well be the outcome. The ideal should be not to maximize the investment and the number of people and area of land engaged in agriculture for the domestic market but to minimize these factors. The more developed a country, the smaller is the proportion of its savings invested in agriculture, the smaller is the percentage of the working force in agriculture and the smaller is agriculture's contribution to the national income. We are in grave danger of confusing what may be a painful necessity forced on us by the growth in population, with something desirable.

Turning to another sector, urban public services, we can all see very clearly how a rapid increase in population calls for ever increasing investment in water, sewerage, energy, traffic facilities and so on. What we perhaps do not see so readily is that, after a certain point, the "solutions" must become ever more costly. We must go further for the water; sewage must be treated; traffic solutions become more and more expensive. I cannot repeat too often that all this absorption of scanty national savings is not to raise the standard of living of the existing population but to supply the same services to additional people.

In trying to meet all these needs of additional people the gap between the standard of living of the masses and the well-to-do people, and between the developed and the underdeveloped peoples grows greater. Dissatisfaction with the existing system and institutions grows. Resort is frequently made to tinkering and improvisation which, in some cases, worsens the functioning of the system and we have another vicious circle. Vicious circles, once they are allowed to become established, require rather heroic measures to break. The problem in Colombia today with eighteen million people is much more difficult of solution than it was in 1951, when there were eleven million. If we do not break the vicious circle of poverty—high birth rates—poverty, it will assuredly be much more difficult in twenty-two years if the population reaches thirty-six million.

So you see why I regard the rate of growth in the population of the underdeveloped countries as the single most important obstacle to development and hence the single most important problem of the world, even outranking in terms of the ultimate dread possibilities, the threat of nuclear warfare. In all underdeveloped countries we desperately need a breathing space, partially freed, for a least a generation, of the ever-growing flood of births in order that we may have a better opportunity to resolve some of the myriad problems that daily grow more acute and unmanageable with the growth in numbers. As Leibenstein so well puts it, restraint of population may not be the *sufficient* condition for development, but it is an *essential* condition.

So far as I know, only one economist of repute, Professor Albert Hirschman, has treated the growth of population as a stimulant in a curious inverted way of its provoking counter pressures and these counter pressures stimulate development, so that he is led to take a "far calmer view of the situation."[11] I suppose he would

11 Albert Hirschman, *The Strategy of Development* (New Haven: Yale University Press, 1958), p. 152.

point to this paper as a manifestation of this counter pressure
or reaction. I confess that I do not relish this role assigned
to me from the Olympian heights of Harvard. Moreover, I would
remind Professor Hirschman that the patient may suffer much
and even die before the countervailing forces are effective.

I have, up to this point, stressed the fertility aspect of the
problem, which applies to both the rich and the poor. But
the rate of population growth is a result of two variables—the
natality and the mortality rates and especially, in the case of the
latter, infant mortality. And here our chief concern must be with
the very poor not only because they are so many but because the
infant mortality rate is still relatively high in this class. The first
and immediate impact of a rise in real income above the subsistence level will probably show itself, therefore, in a decline in
mortality rates, or what Harvey Leibenstein calls an induced
rate of population growth. Something like this appears to be
happening in many underdeveloped countries. The first impact
of preventive medicine and more food is a decline in mortality
rates and an actual growth in the rate of population increase.
In Colombia, this may have been as much as fifty percent in the
thirteen years from 1951 to 1964.

Various studies suggest that after a period and if the income
rise is sufficiently large and especially if people find profitable
work in the cities, the fall in mortality rate is overcome and
more than overcome by the fall in natality rates. For this reason
we cannot afford to take the long view and become too com-
placent with the success of relatively small and isolated efforts.
We must never forget the sheer magnitude or the arithmetic of
the problem. It is not true that as long as the growth in average
per capita income exceeds the rate of growth in population,
eventual development is assured. The growth in per capita income may correspond with a worsening of the condition of the
poorest; the rate of population growth can further increase with
a decline in mortality rates; the best natural resources are already
exploited; per capita savings and investment may decline; the
functioning of our economic and political institutions may

worsen. In short, it would be highly imprudent to place our faith, in a matter of this importance, in simple arithmetic formulus. While, in a country like Colombia, we are necessarily thinking in terms of the education of a few thousand urban mothers, we must not forget the 700,000 odd births a year in the country at large, and that this figure will almost certainly grow in the next few years unless truly herculean efforts are made and are successful.

Viewed in the perspective of this paper, the things that daily occupy the headlines and the radio commentaries appear relatively unimportant. They concern more the consequences of the loss of control over our environment than the basic causes. Unfortunately, it is difficult to arouse and maintain interest in a problem that is with us from day to day and year to year. But we must try, and devote an ever larger share of our resources to the study and the solution of the problem. For that reason I cannot applaud too heartily the pioneering work of the Population Council, the Population Reference Bureau and the other public spirited groups that are working on the problem. I hope that the day is not far distant when official national development plans also include in their objectives a marked reduction in the rate of population growth.

VI

Technology and the Problem of the Mix in Underdeveloped Countries

The most puzzling and indeed baffling aspect of the continuance of underdevelopment is its coincidence with accessibility to growing technology. The same technology that permits some 2 percent of the American work force to produce 75 percent of its agricultural harvests (including enormous exports) is in large part as least available or accessible to the underdeveloped world; as are the marvels of industrial technology. An underdeveloped country today does not have to retrace the painful steps of the Industrial Revolution where the machines enabled their operators to produce little more per day than the hand work of their predecessors. Just as they can pass from the mule to the jet so they can pass from the hoe to the tractor and from the sickle to the combine. Confronted with these possibilities, one would naturally expect that development would be much more rapid than in the earlier or even present stages of developed economies. While the United States is moving increasingly toward the provision of services, the underdeveloped world has the opportunity to accelerate the production of goods of mass consumption, in which generally the economies of scale are most striking. Certainly an explanation is required.

A first approach to an explanation may be made by reviewing the striking characteristics of development in the nineteenth century. By and large, throughout this long period of time the market or price system functioned in accordance with modern textbook theory. Sufficient incentives were provided to work, to shift jobs, to save, to invest, to improve or to innovate. The mobility mechanism (with some notable exceptions) functioned sufficiently well to permit an "economic" allocation of new savings and a steady shift of workers to better paying jobs.[1] The growth of population, except in the United States, was sufficiently low (1 percent a year or a doubling every seventy-five years or so) not to place too heavy a load on the mobility mechanism. This became especially true in the United States after the restriction of immigration. The annual growth in labor-saving, capital-intensive improvements, except in agriculture for a period in this century, was again such that its combination with labor—the composition of the mix—could keep pace with it. The decline in price competition and the growth in trade unions and minimum wage legislation was delayed to a time when new fields were rapidly opening up so that cost-push inflation became important more as a factor bearing on a country's competitive position than as a cause of continuing unemployment. The result was that the transition was made from labor-abundant, capital-scarce economies to capital-abundant, labor-scarce ones in a relatively smooth and continuous process. No violent or sudden change in the mix was required.

The exceptions to this sweeping statement are significant. One was the Great Depression. The price system did not react quickly enough and a point was passed when a decline in aggregate demand resulted in a further decline—a vicious circle was established which was only finally and assuredly broken by the Second World War and the structural changes in the system induced by the war and postwar developments. Another highly significant exception was to be found in the Cotton South where the mix remained highly unfavorable to labor for one hundred fifty years.

1 See Chapter IX in this volume on Mobility and Output.

The explanation of this particular vicious circle and the events that brought about its end are again to be found in profound institutional factors working, it is true, through the price system, but nevertheless institutional. Similar vicious circles still exist in the continuance of Appalachia and the city slums—situations whose correction resist the operation of market forces and appear to call for institutional changes.

A third and highly instructive evident change in the mix occurred during and immediately after the Second World War. In the United States, with the slack that prevailed in 1939 and the need for utilizing key equipment in second and third shifts the ratio of employment to capital undoubtedly rose. In Western Europe, immediately after the war, reliance was not had on the price mechanism to bring about a violent change in the mix in the form of a great increase in workers per dollar of investment. Rather, the United States underwrote an enormous exchange deficit for the three or four years that it took Western Europe to reestablish the previous mix and even increase the investment, at least in terms of productive capacity per unit of labor. One might quibble whether this was an institutional change but at least it was not reliance on the market mechanism to bring about the desired change in the mix.

It should now be apparent that utilizing the techniques of capital-abundant economies in labor-abundant economies poses peculiarly difficult problems of varying the mix. How to insure that a few workers in petro-chemical plants or refineries do not dispose of relatively enormous amounts of capital per worker, while most workers have none? That a relatively few mechanized farms do not result in an extension of subsistence farming? That capital imports do not result in disguised unemployment, which is an underdeveloped country's equivalent to technological unemployment? In such cases modern technology could become a curse instead of a blessing, as it has in permitting a fall in the death rate far in advance of any fall in the birth rate.

Various solutions come to mind. A Chicago-trained or influenced economist would probably immediately ask why not give the market mechanism a chance to vary the mix appropriately by letting the price of imported capital goods soar in a free or floating exchange market and by letting wage rates fall to whatever point is necessary to assume full employment? A more complete answer to this suggested course of action is provided in another essay in this volume.[2]

Here we may mention that we are dealing with existing situations where extreme inequality of income and lack of confidence in the future are hard facts. A floating free rate may result in a dissipation of scanty exchange resources in luxury imports, capital imports to make luxury goods, foreign travel and foreign education, and a chronic flight of capital. The price mechanism is only a mechanism. It works as blindly to satisfy the effective demands of the few rich as the many poor. The lower level on wages may be provided by subsistence farming. It is a poor solution if we have to resort to Professor Schultz's rigid definitions to insist that such people are all "employed"—a semantic rather than a substantive solution. In this case, it will be seen that the market or price economists are assuming a certain set of institutional factors—a tolerable degree of income equality, confidence, a free labor market—in order that the market mechanism may provide a solution to an admitted economic problem.

In the case of Colombia a high rate of exchange would enormously benefit the larger and more prosperous coffee growers. The resulting greatly increased planting and production would either have to be sternly repressed or the breakdown of the World Coffee Pact would result in a long price war in a commodity with both a highly inelastic demand and little response of supply to a drastic fall in price.

A second type of solution was once rather casually suggested by Professor Kuznets to the effect that underdeveloped countries should modify the capital-intensive equipment to make it less so. But how? Some writers have pointed to the example of Japan, where, it is stated, agriculture improvement for many years took the form of varieties and cultural practices rather than

[2] On Foreign Economic Policy.

equipment. This is theoretically possible in a few fields. It requires a good deal of discipline and sophistication if it is not to result in the Mexican solution of a technically backward, overabundant peasantry.

It is difficult to change the design of a refinery or synthetic fibre plant to use more labor and less capital equipment. Somewhat more flexibility is possible in agriculture provided, as often happens, labor codes do not stand in the way. Even here, one cannot use two drivers in a tractor at the same time, although a change in the Labor Code (and labor discipline!) might make a twenty-four hour operation feasible.

It must be admitted that the market system does try, despite the institutional obstacles, to make the appropriate response. The family farm can contract for tractor custom work and work long hours to compete with the commercial type farm struggling with labor problems; the same occurs in the persistence of numberless small workshops in the electrical, metal and wood working fields in the larger cities, utilizing more labor per dollar of investment, again because of peculiar problems relating to the use of labor. On the other hand, these same problems may lead to a substitution of machines for hand work in the larger factories, thus working against what might be regarded as a more appropriate mix. Freezing of rents, common in underdeveloped countries, may lead to the building of apartments and offices to sell and not to rent.

The argument I am trying to develop is not that a less unfettered price system might not in itself work toward a better mix, even given the existence of capital equipment developed for capital-abundant economies. It is rather that this better mix, given conditions of gross inequality and the difficulty underdeveloped countries, just because they are underdeveloped, experience in developing exports, makes it probable that a dual economy of considerable magnitude can continue to exist even if more reliance is had on the price mechanism.

But such an economy, even in a country with such a favorable balance of payments as Mexico, can lead to a perpetuation of the vicious circle of high birth rates—low educational standards and poverty in over half of the population—in other words, to conditions making a desirable mix almost impossible to attain without wise and massive aid being given to the market mechanism.

The mechanism, in other words, cannot be that of gradually equipping more and more workers with the same complement of capital goods appropriate to a capital-abundant society while drawing down the "pool" of unequipped "surplus" workers, for the simple reason that the pool is being fed more rapidly than this process can reduce it, so that, after many years of trial, its level is today far higher than it was at the beginning of the process. This, if valid, is a conclusion of enormous practical importance as it suggests that the theoretical base of the various programs to overcome underdevelopment is inadequate. The problem of underdevelopment has become one that cannot be resolved even by a perfectly functioning market system; more important are its dynamic and institutional elements that call for an approach widely different from the current extension of limited loans and grants and technical assistance.

A corollary conclusion is that the favorite solution of all underdeveloped countries—an improvement in the balance of payments resulting either from borrowing or by exports—can rarely be of the magnitude that would permit a pattern of consumption and a type of mix appropriate in the developed countries. Mexico and Venezuela are cases in point. Additional gross capital in the private sector alone per additional worker in the United States for the period 1956-64 amounted to $75,000. The pattern and volume of consumption and the type of capital goods that resulted reflected, of course, this change in the mix.

A factor aggravating the inadequacy of capital in relation to labor is the generally shocking underutilization of existing capital and malallocation of new capital. This underutilization and malallocation in both the private and public sector is made up of a large number of factors which could be the subject of another essay. It may suffice to say that underdevelopment is generally an all-pervasive phenomenon touching every aspect of a country's life. The poor use of capital is a symptom of underdevelopment as well as a cause—just one of the many vicious circles that impede the effective functioning of the market system.

There is, however, a theoretical escape from our apparent dilemma. Admitting that imports of capital goods are limited and inadequate in relation to the growing labor force, could not an unfettered price system lead to the production of capital goods internally so that a better mix can be obtained by using more of the unemployed (disguised) in making capital goods? This possibility could be combined with institutional modifications that would make profitable the far more intensive use of existing and newly imported capital goods, as in wartime. In these two ways, a better mix for the economy as a whole, or a higher complement of capital per worker, could be attained. The combination of these two lines of attack could, I have argued elsewhere, if pursued sufficiently massively and persistently, be the answer to our problem.

The addition to domestically made capital could take the form of construction of all types, particularly multiple housing in the larger cities. Housing, fortunately, is still accepted as a capital rather than as a consumer good and yields its actual or imputed rent immediately upon occupation. It has a high labor input and a low imported capital component. A large volume can, at least in theory, be produced by taking up some of the tremendous slack in the system. Thus the mix can be improved by actual underemployed labor and capital being put to work to produce new capital (and goods of mass consumption).

All visitors to Caracas are impressed by the number of new, high-rise apartment buildings and carelessly assume that this is another manifestation of the petroleum bonanza. In a way, of course, it is but the relation is not the simple, direct one commonly assumed. Oil revenues created conditions favorable to such construction. The overwhelming part of the construction, however, was done by Venezuelan labor and management using Venezuelan raw material, while much of the income from petroleum exports was expended in the import of consumer goods and many capital goods of doubtful value. What came about indirectly and almost absentmindedly (apartment building never had high priority in a national plan) could be directly planned by a country that wanted to achieve a better mix while confronted with an inadequate supply of capital-intensive capital goods incorporating advanced techniques, and a vast supply of labor.

However, as was argued earlier, the removal of restraints on prices and competition would not bring this about automatically as long as other factors making for a malallocation of capital are left untouched. The underlying situation has deteriorated to such an extent in many underdeveloped countries (lack of confidence, flight of capital, inequality in incomes and opportunity, labor and other monopolies, and so on) that a new set of controls and institutional changes would be necessary to enable the price mechanism to vary the mix sufficiently. The extent and magnitude of these changes and the fact that some of them would encounter bitter opposition as being either radical or retrogressive, make their enactment highly unlikely unless laid down as a condition of the receipt of massive aid. This could be tried out initially in a pilot country.

Clearly, to utilize capital-intensive equipment and provide more remunerative employment in general with limited imports is a problem requiring careful study by each underdeveloped country. All that can be done here is to suggest a few general lines of policy and criteria for establishing priorities.

(a) In the first place every effort should be made to use the market mechanism as far as it is feasible. This implies relatively high prices for imported capital goods and a relatively low level of wages and salaries as long as a great amount of disguised unemployment exists.

(b) Under the conditions prevailing in many underdeveloped countries, quantitative restrictions on the purchase of foreign currency may be necessary to offset the effects of great inequality of income and lack of confidence. In applying rationing, the most difficult decisions will arise as between goods permitting future exports (or substitution of imports), public services, and goods permitting production of goods of mass consumption (including housing). Most public services are also mass consumption goods. However, too low costs and tariffs may encourage extravagant use as indicated by abnormally high growth rates in the consumption of electricity in relation to the growth in industrial use. Many imports for future exports or to substitute for other imports have in practice not done so and such justifications must be critically examined.

(c) Even in the mass consumption industries, high intensity of use should be given high priority in permitting imports.

(d) Something can be done in reducing imported capital requirements without loss of essential services. City planning that reduces transit and transport requirements is an example, as would be the substitution of express and exclusive bus-ways at peak hours in place of the use of private cars.

(e) Avoidance of patterns of consumption whose widespread adoption presupposes a capital-abundant economy would make for a better factor mix for the community as a whole. These include not only individually expensive items such as cars, but also the costly systems of processing and packaging goods that have grown up in developed countries. Examples would be the throw-away paper milk cartons and a host of plastic containers.

(f) Probably, too much emphasis has been given the infrastructure. We forget that the developed countries advanced far on the road to development with a minimum of public expenditures. The art of maintaining good dirt roads has been almost forgotten. In Colombia a much more intensive use of the railroad could mean a large saving in foreign exchange entailed by long haul trucking. Construction of elaborate irrigation works while there is still an abundance of good land with adequate rainfall is another instance. Yet imports for these purposes are universally accorded highest priority.

It should be kept in mind that these are only general suggestions. Obtaining a more desirable factor mix obviously depends on the actual mix, the degree of inequality in income, the foreign balance and other factors, which vary from country to country. It is suggested, however, that we have here an important part of the explanation of the persistence of dual economies, which is only another way of saying massive disguised unemployment or very poor mobility, which in turn is an important part of the explanation of self-perpetuating underdevelopment.

VII

Disguised Unemployment and Saving-Investment

Few economic concepts have been subject to as much hostile criticism and yet have continued to be so extensively used as that of disguised unemployment. Since Mrs. Robinson first invented the phrase in 1936,[1] it has been repeatedly assailed. Its persistent and unrelenting critic, Professor T. W. Schultz, demolished it in 1956[2] but felt it necessary to repeat the job in 1964.[3] Drs. Charles H. C. Kao, Kurt R. Anschel and Carl K. Eicher reviewed its life history in 1964 and formally pronounced it dead.[4] It was again "disproved" by Dr. Morton Paglin in 1965.[5] However, Mrs.

[1] Joan Robinson, "Disguised Unemployment," *Economic Journal*, Vol. 46, June 1936, pp. 225-237.

[2] T. W. Schultz, "The Role of Government in Promoting Economic Growth" in Leonard D. White (ed.) *The State of the Social Sciences* (Chicago: University of Chicago Press, 1956), pp. 372-383.

[3] T. W. Schultz, "The Doctrine of Agricultural Labor of Zero Value," *Transforming Traditional Agriculture* (New Haven: Yale University Press, 1964).

[4] Charles H. C. Kao, Kurt R. Anschel and Carl K. Eicher, "Disguised Unemployment in Agriculture: A Survey," Carl K. Eicher and Lawrence W. Witt (eds.) in *Agriculture in Economic Development* (New York: McGraw-Hill Book Co., 1964), pp. 129-144.

[5] Morton Paglin, "Surplus Agricultural Labor and Development: Facts and Theories," *American Economic Review*, Sept., 1965, pp. 815-834.

Robinson's concept appears to be too useful to be thus disposed of and undoubtedly will be around for a long time to come. This paper is an attempt to explain why.

I

NATURE AND SIGNIFICANCE OF THE CONCEPT

As Kao, Anschel and Eicher quite rightly point out, the existence or non-existence of disguised unemployment is largely a matter of definition. Some of the writers who have used the term (but not Mrs. Robinson) defined it as labor with zero marginal productivity that therefore could be dispensed with without any loss in output. Other writers (especially the critics) have interpreted this definition as precluding any technical advances or changes in factor proportions even over time. So shackled by definition, it has not been difficult to demonstrate that such unemployment cannot exist in theory, and defenders have unwarily allowed themselves to accept these shackles and have expended considerable ingenuity in imagining how a member of a peasant family may produce nothing but receive something. This is surprising, as even elementary texts usually discuss the ambiguities and conceptual difficulties inherent in the concept of both employment and unemployment.

Fortunately there is no Royal Academy in economics to insist on rigid definitions of words, as in Spain, and, at least within limits, we all can be Humpty Dumptys in making words mean what we want them to mean.

Disguised Unemployment and Development

It seems to me that the definition adopted should be one that is significant and useful for purposes of analysis. From this point of view, insistence on "labor of zero productivity" deprives the concept of any significance, since such labor hardly exists. By the same token such a definition would likewise deprive the word "unemployment" itself of much of its usefulness as we would have to exclude all the workers out of regular work who occupied themselves in odd jobs, even around their house or garden, and in casual labor. Surely our interest should be not in setting up straw men in order to knock them down, but rather in advancing our understanding of economic phenomena.

Professor Viner is, I believe, the only writer who went to the heart of the matter and discussed the concept in terms of its usefulness.[6] True, he accepted the rigid and restrictive definition of others in criticizing their use of the concept but in his conclusion he suggested a more reasonable definition and pointed the way to a fruitful approach. "At this admittedly tentative stage of my thinking, however, I am tempted to conclude that there is little or nothing in all the phenomena designated as 'disguised unemployment' as 'hidden unemployment' or as 'underemployment' which in so far as they constitute genuine social problems would not be adequately taken into account by competent, informed, and comprehensive analysis of the phenomena of low productivity of employed labor, its causes, its true extent and its possible remedies."[7] I would draw the reader's attention to the criterion of "social problems," to the substitution of "low productivity"[8] for "zero productivity" and to the introduction of the considerations of causes, extent and remedies of such low productivity. This transfers the whole discussion from one dangerously close to word chopping to one concerned with significant phenomena. As one who has made extensive use of the concept

6 Jacob Viner, "Some Reflections on the Concept of Disguised Unemployment," *The Indian Journal of Economics,* July 1957, pp. 17-23.

7 *Ibid.,* p. 23.

8 Curiously, Kao, Anschel and Eicher demolish their own argument by letting three little words slip in that change completely their original rigidly constraining definition of zero productivity. After asking why wages should be higher than the marginal product, they go on to say that "If large numbers of people produce nothing *or very little,* wages normally would be bid down to the marginal product of labor," Kao, Anschel and Eicher, p. 132. Italics added. In subsistence agriculture the product and the wages are indeed *very little.*

of "disguised unemployment"[9] and has found it most helpful, I feel constrained to defend my usage and try to convince Professor Viner that the concept does help us in treating of "social problems."

Let me first concede that, defining the concept in terms of labor with (relatively) low productivity, Professor Viner is perfectly right in a formal sense. My reasons for preferring the terms "disguised" and "underemployment" or "underutilization of human resources" are rather for expository and semantic reasons. The agriculture of most of the Latin American countries is characterized by a dual structure—a numerically small section of relatively efficient, technically advanced and/or mechanized farming on the one hand and primitive colonial type farming on the other. The latter shades into subsistence farming, where the most urgent problems of underdevelopment in terms of poverty, ignorance and high birth rates are concentrated. I have found again and again, not only in my own thinking but in that of others, that to talk of farmers with low productivity or with productivity approaching zero evokes an entirely different reaction than to refer to such agriculturalists as the disguised unemployed. Our conditioned reflex to low productivity is to think immediately in terms of ways and means to increase productivity *in agriculture*, which probably is the basic reason why so many trained economists, even at this late date, fall victims of the fallacy of composition and advocate measures to increase the productivity of fifty percent or more of the working population who are in agriculture. On the other hand, to refer to the colonial type sector as constituting the disguised unemployed evokes the reaction of where and how we can find employment for them. Thus, from the point of view of Professor Viner's criteria of explaining social problems and in discussing the causes, extent and remedies of such problems, a strong case can be made for the use of the words disguised or underemployment. It would be a grave mistake to minimize the importance of semantics, as

[9] Lauchlin Currie, *Accelerating Development: The Necessity and the Means* (New York: McGraw-Hill Book Co., 1966), pp. 178-183.

much of economics is concerned with our efforts to communicate.

It may be objected that if we substitute the words "relatively low" for "zero" productivity we cannot at the same time maintain that such labor can be replaced without loss of production. But this is true only as of a given moment of time and by ruling out the possibility of accelerating the introduction of technical advances or changing the factor proportions over a relatively short time. If our interest is in real problems rather than in scoring debaters' points, we would be more concerned with the elasticity of supply of production in the commercial agricultural sector that could replace the production of the colonial type sector, if it paid to do so. It must be recognized that the production of the latter sector, though it may yield a miserable income, nevertheless operates to keep the price of produce down and to this extent discourages the conversion to known and practiced technical advances and mechanization in the commercial sector. The more successful we are in raising the physical productivity of the peasants on small uneconomic sized farms, the more we will delay the adoption of the most advanced agricultural practices. It is literally impossible for fifty percent of the workers to produce food *efficiently* for themselves and the other fifty percent unless the population is excessively large in relation to resources. Surely the important thing, therefore, is not to demonstrate that if, at a given moment, a peasant is producing *something* he cannot be displaced without a loss of production—this follows from definition and does not need an empirical demonstration—but rather to concentrate on studies on the elasticity of supply in commercial agriculture where such a type of agriculture exists side by side with a primitive non-technical type of agriculture, and on the increase in production that would result from a better distribution of the work force.

But, it may still further be objected, it is impossible to measure such elasticity precisely or to determine how many and over what time the low productivity farmers could be displaced without loss of production and without an excessive rise in prices of agricultural products. All this I would concede but I would still defend the use of the phrase "disguised unemployment." Even that most sacred of all sacred cows, the G.N.P., is fuzzy conceptually and its measurement rests on very arbitrary decisions. I would maintain that for policy purposes in dealing with the problem of underdevelopment, the problems posed by the existence of a primitive, semi-subsistence type of agriculture are so urgent and the numbers of persons involved are so large, that great precision is not necessary. The edges of most concepts in the social sciences are blurred but we do not stop using them for that reason. Why insist on such precision in the case of disguised unemployment or, as Professor Viner would prefer to say, employment with very low productivity?

In my recent book[10] I used some simple calculations based on Colombian statistics for 1960 to convey an impression of the tremendous slack in the system or of the amount of labor that might be classified as constituting the disguised unemployed in agriculture (or labor with very low productivity). These calculations were designed to throw some light on the questions of what would be the land and labor requirement to produce the harvests of 1960 if (a) all such crops that lent themselves to mechanization were produced by the type of commercial farming that actually existed in Colombia in that year in those crops, with the average yields that were estimated to prevail in that type of farming, and (b) if coffee, which is not subject to mechanization in Colombia, were produced in economic-sized units averaging five hectares instead of the tiny holdings that characterize the cultivation of much of this crop. Under these assumptions it was calculated that the labor force in agriculture could have been reduced from fifty-two percent to fourteen percent of the total labor force, while the area under cultivation could have been reduced by one half.

This calculation was rough and could undoubtedly be refined, and the basic data leave much to be desired. No attempt was made to estimate the additional food requirements of displaced agriculturalists. It does not pretend to say that thirty-eight per-

10 *Ibid.*, pp. 168-186.

cent of the labor force could be withdrawn overnight from agriculture without loss of production. All it was designed to indicate was that, with the extension of the modest type of technification that was actually known and practiced in the country and a consolidation of coffee holdings to a modest extent, a tremendous pool of labor would become available for the production of other non-agricultural products and services. Probably the figure would be less today as the population is growing at such an alarming rate. On the other hand, the numbers in colonial and subsistence type farming continue to grow and presumably technical advances in agriculture are continuing.

The indicated "surplus" of nearly forty percent of the working force in 1960 in agriculture alone was most certainly not a measure of disguised unemployment as the critics would like to define the term. Nevertheless it would appear to be a highly significant and provocative calculation from the point of view of the diagnosis of underdevelopment and the selection of strategies, or, in Professors Viner's terms, "the cause, extent and remedies" of widespread and extremely low productivity of the employed. I doubt very much if the same diagnosis and strategy would be suggested by the statement that seventy-three percent of the labor force in agriculture in 1960 had very low productivity.

The significant datum in development, as in calculating the magnitude of a possible effort in war time, is not the actual listed unemployed or even the numbers that could be released overnight without loss of production, but rather the slack in the system that could be utilized through a feasible change in the resource-mix and changes in the patterns of production and consumption. Such a calculation poses not only the magnitude of the problem of development but also the potential opportunity to increase production greatly.

Viewed from the standpoint of this paper, Professor Schultz's ingenious citation of the presumed repercussions of the influenza epidemic of 1918 in India on the following year's acreage sown, in which little time was allowed for the rearrangement of factors nor allowance made for the fact that that particular epidemic struck down the healthiest and most robust, appears irrelevant. In any case, the percentage decline in area sown was much less than the decline in the agricultural labor force. An empirical disproof of disguised unemployment in India offered by Dr. Morton Paglin[11] rests on a small sample that indicates that yields *per acre* are higher in small than in larger farms, as might have been expected. In only one case are days of work per acre given and this indicates that the labor productivity falls as farms become smaller. If this is truly a case where there is grave overpopulation and all suitable land is under cultivation and it is a matter of life and death to produce more food per acre and the productivity per man has ceased to be important and better techniques are not available, the situation is indeed desperate and we may concede that there may be no hope of releasing workers from agriculture. My knowledge of India does not permit me to make a judgment though I note that Dr. Paglin expressly rules out of consideration changes in the resource-mix in agriculture, whereas Professor Reddaway, an authority on India, maintains that "the increase in [agricultural] output depends preponderantly on the introduction of better methods."[12] Why, then, not advocate changes in this instead of a further increase in the man-land ratio? In any case, I would insist that these conditions do not as yet apply to Latin American countries, although they could in the not distant future if the rate of population growth is not slowed. Paradoxically, the crux of the population problem can be found in the large mass of very poor and ignorant country people whom I have called the disguised unemployed and for whom it is urgent to find remunerative employment before they become actually needed in agriculture, which will signify that we have already lost the race against time and population growth.

The problem appears to me to be one of extreme urgency. To insist that there is no disguised unemployed with the corollary that no workers can be released from agriculture is to court the

11 Paglin, *op. cit.*, pp. 815-834.
12 W. B. Reddaway, "The Economics of Underdeveloped Countries," *Economic Journal*, March, 1963, p. 5.

danger of making a wrong diagnosis, adopting the wrong remedies and losing the battle of population pressure and, in the apt
words of Professor Leibenstein, to fail to make the critical
minimum effort necessary to cut short the lengthening fertility
lag and attain a level from which self-sustaining growth is possible. The issue far transcends definitions and semantics. It is at
the heart of the underdevelopment problem.

II

DISGUISED UNEMPLOYMENT AND THE
KEYNESIAN ANALYSIS

It is possible that the widespread criticism of the disguised
unemployed concept originates in part from the success of the
Keynesian Revolution. Since, in the *General Theory,* the only
explanation offered of unemployment is an excessive propensity
to save in relation to incentives to invest at levels of income
that correspond with full employment, one is naturally suspicious
of or hostile to a concept of unemployment not readily explicable
in Keynesian terms, and particularly mass unemployment.[13] There
is one additional source of open unemployment that most economists recognize, that arising from the efforts to maintain price
stability in the face of cost-push or sellers' inflation. This, however, in developed countries is usually a very small percentage
of the labor force and the main concern over cost-push inflation
is that it may weaken a country's competitive position in world
trade.

If, then, we persist in the use of the concept of disguised un-

[13] Although Keynes clearly recognized the possibility of unemployment
arising from a "too high" level of costs and prices [in the *Economic Consequences of Mr. Churchill* and in a reference in the *General Theory* (p.
269) to Australian legal minimum wages] he tended to think of this in relation to a country's foreign trade position. Both his semi-inflation and true or
absolute inflation cases arise from prior increases in aggregate buying power
(*General Theory,* pp. 301-302). This is curious, as when he wrote the *General
Theory* he must have had before him the N.R.A. cost-push inflation of 1933-
34 and its consequences.

employment, what can we offer as the explanation of such unemployment? Since we have already agreed that the concept could, in a formal sense, correspond with the employed with relatively very low productivity, our explanation must also be applicable to such employed. Clearly, a first approximation that would fit both cases would run in terms of a faulty functioning of the labor mobility factor or a breakdown in the human resource allocation mechanism. A test of such faulty functioning would be a wide (and possibly growing) disparity in earnings within the working force to an extent that cannot be accounted for in terms of differences in regional living costs or disagreeableness of the work. In Latin American countries we find such wide and in many cases growing differences between the earnings of the industrial workers and white collar workers on the one hand and the urban casual workers and the rural workers on the other.

Lack of adequate mobility itself, however, requires explanations. Part of the explanation, I believe, can be found in the familiar concept of cost-push inflation. Industry, in Latin American countries, is dominated by relatively few units and is unionized. Independent empirical studies in Colombia by Dr. Albert Berry and by the author indicate that real wages of unionized labor rose markedly from 1955 to 1962 in relation to non-unionized and particularly rural labor.[14] This is also consistent with developments in Colombia from the end of 1961 to the close of 1965. The cost of living index rose from 176 to 314 while reported industrial employment remained unchanged, despite the rapid growth in the labor force and continuous migration to cities and, in general, a sustained volume of capital goods imports. Throughout this period the rise in industrial real wages in general preceded the rise in the cost of living index. It is true that the industrial sector is relatively small but growth in this sector is the dynamic factor in generating employment in the related and larger fields of transport, commerce and factory and office construction. The growth in city slums in this period suggests that while there was movement of labor, there was a lack of adequate mobility.

[14] Currie, pp. 193-195, 204.

Another part of the explanation may be found in the labor-economizing nature of capital imports. In the period 1951-64 in Colombia a technical revolution in agriculture occurred accompanied by a transport revolution which made new areas with rich alluvial soils accessible to the rapidly growing cities. The marked rise in agricultural output must have been accounted for almost wholly by the rapidly growing commercial type sector of agriculture. The condition of the colonial type farmers, whose numbers continued to increase in absolute terms, probably worsened with further subdivision of holdings and growth in the number of squatters. Again, a case of insufficient mobility to permit adequate adjustment to technical advances and the rapid increase in the labor force.

The Keynesian explanation of employment and unemployment purports to be a *general* theory. An interesting question, therefore, is whether disguised unemployment (or a poor distribution of the working force) or cost-push unemployment or technological unemployment can be explained in terms of the saving-investment analysis. Can it be demonstrated that disguised unemployment or a very poor distribution of the employed is a consequence of an excessive propensity to save?

At first, such a question appears a little absurd. Is not inadequate saving and a desperate shortage of capital equipment or investment a universal characteristic of underdeveloped countries? However, "inadequate" and "shortage" are relative terms. If cost-push or sellers' inflation is sufficiently widespread and severe and there are official or institutional discouragements to the intensive use of equipment such as surcharges for night work, a "shortage" of equipment in comparison with wealthy countries may be converted into an "excess" of productive capacity in relation to its use, paradoxical as this may seem. In Colombia, even when prices are rising rapidly, the stores are well stocked with goods *at a price,* and much industrial equipment continues to be worked at only ten to fifteen percent of the hours of the year. As a protective measure and for quick profits, investment in inventories may appear more attractive than investment in additional productive capacity. Sluggish sales in terms of physical volume resulting from excessive mark-ups may actually discourage growth in physical production, employment and investment in capital equipment.

Extreme inequality in income, by permitting consumer expenditures abroad and the flight of capital for security or speculative purposes, may cause leakages in the circular stream of money income which would have the same effect on internal employment as would a propensity to save not matched by incentives to invest at home.

It could be argued that in 1932-33 in the United States the wage and price level was "too high" to permit greater sales, production and employment (though it does not follow that, as of that time, a reduction would have led to increased employment), so that this explanation gives the same result as saying that at the income and price levels of 1932-33 the propensity to save (even though actual savings were negative) was too high in relation to incentives to invest, to provide more employment or, more reasonably, that consumption was "too low." Similarly, it can be argued that in an underdeveloped country the propensity to save is too high, or consumption is too low, to assure full employment (or a better distribution of the "employed"). Thus, in an admittedly somewhat strained sense, disguised unemployment might be explained in terms of the Keynesian analysis.

The post-Keynesians, in arguing for the necessity of a higher propensity to save and a reduced propensity to consume in underdeveloped countries appear to be misapplying the Keynesian analysis from the point of view of observed phenomena of unemployment (open and disguised) and underutilization of equipment, and for policy purposes. However, it should be noted that under existing conditions, any attempt to increase consumption by increasing aggregate money demand would probably be promptly stultified or offset by sellers' inflation. It would appear wiser, therefore, not to try to use the Keynesian approach and rather to deal directly with the more basic causes of the lack of adequate mobility. The Keynesian analysis would seem to be much better adapted to deal with money aggregates and not to lend itself readily to the explanation of the consequences of conditions of imperfect competition, technological unemployment, chronic inflation, extreme inequality of incomes and various institutional factors that prevail in many underdeveloped countries.

A significant by-product of the identification of disguised unemployment with the low income employed is the finding that cost-push inflation and other factors that impede mobility can be the cause of a poor distribution of the working force as well as unemployment, both open and disguised. It is more difficult to recognize this dual consequence in the United States because of the existence of countervailing power restraining sellers' inflation, the dynamic growth of the generally non-unionized and competitive service fields and the rise in educational standards, all of which have contributed to a high degree of labor mobility as indicated by the trend toward equality in earnings. For faulty functioning of the mobility mechanism in the United States one must now turn to city slums and Appalachia, for which special explanations are necessary, some of them being basically noneconomic in nature.

In this lecture I have sought to defend the concept of disguised unemployment on expository grounds by freeing it from the shackles of unduly rigid definitions, by identifying it with the employed with relatively very low productivity, and by showing its relation to the distribution of the labor force and inadequate mobility. Unemployment in this sense can be explained in Keynesian terms but on the whole it would appear preferable not to try to use Keynesian analysis in seeking to diagnose the problem of underdevelopment or in selecting appropriate strategies to cope with that problem. By identifying the concept of disguised unemployment with the employed earning very low incomes it is seen that much of the explanation of unemployment, open and disguised, is also the explanation of a poor distribution of the work force in underdeveloped countries.

VIII

Underdevelopment and Foreign Trade and Exchange Policy[*]

The article by Professor Johnson is a modern and sophisticated statement of the traditional liberal position in economic policy, extended to underdeveloped economies. Government intervention is almost certainly likely to be ill-conceived and inefficient and to result in distortions in the economic system (as measured by departures from the allocation of resources that would result from the play of market forces). The exceptions to this general attitude are to be found where natural forces do not produce a satisfactory result—a progressive income tax to correct for inequalities in income, monetary control to provide neutrality in the price system, a floating exchange rate where monetary control is ineffective, and presumably certain forms of price control where monopoly elements exist and where, for one reason

* This paper was originally written as a commentary on Harry Johnson's article on Fiscal Policy and the Balance of Payments in a Growth Economy, which article first appeared in the *Malaya Economic Review*, Vol. IX, No. 1, 1964. I worked from an offprint which did not contain the original page references.

and another, competition cannot be restored, and, more recently, deliberate manipulation of aggregate demand to maintain full employment. By and large, development planning is conceived as providing the social infrastructure and as removing obstacles to the efficient functioning of the economic system in its classical capitalistic form, as just indicated.

Perhaps too much should not be made of this point since, as with all economies, it is a matter of degree and emphasis. Many forms of intervention, especially in underdeveloped countries, are ill-conceived and badly executed. The mixed system of economic organization, as it has evolved in economically advanced countries, does insure a reasonably intensive use of productive factors and a pattern of production-consumption and/or a corresponding allocation of resources consistent with consumer demand under conditions of full employment. It is natural, therefore, that economists of developed countries should share a common bias in favor of the traditional liberal position, as modified in developed countries. The presumption generally is for what exists, is working reasonably well, and is known and more or less understood. Moreover, as technicians, economists are naturally fascinated by the silent, intricate functioning of the price system in all its myriad manifestations.

While, therefore, I sympathize with the liberal position, though not with some of the extreme applications of the Chicago School, nevertheless I think that in dealing with development policies we must be acutely aware of the assumptions, biases and prejudices, mostly implicit, underlying our approach. I fear that Professor Johnson, in the preparation of the present paper, was insufficiently aware of these assumptions and biases.

Many points are touched upon in this paper. In general, however, the policy advice proffered to underdeveloped countries is against exchange rationing, import-substitution, multiple exchange rates and departures from "equilibrium" rates of exchange, and is in favor of "equilibrium" rates (floating rates or as frequent devaluations as necessary to maintain "equilibrium" in the balance of payments), and fiscal measures of general applicability. If the actual rate of exchange departs from the equilibrium, the authorities should calculate the rate that corresponds with equilibrium and use this shadow rate in the application of specific measures to avoid distortion in the allocation of resources. But this is offered as a second-best policy. In general, the advice in the exchange field is adherence to the free-trade, neutral or equilibrium exchange rate policy and against manipulations in this field designed to further development.

It is difficult to take issue with Professor Johnson if we accept his assumptions. They are not all explicitly mentioned but they seem to be as follows:

1) underdeveloped countries have a bias toward inflation and chronic unbalance in their external payments;

2) their economies are operating at full capacity under existing conditions of techniques;

3) in the absence of ill-conceived interventions, the distribution of factors of production would be the optimum in view of available resources, i.e. the pricing mechanism and the mobility mechanism are functioning efficiently;

4) the distribution of income is irrelevent to any judgment on the efficiency of the resource allocation mechanism;

5) curiously enough and in apparent contradiction with item (3) above, government expenditures are more favorable to development than private expenditures.

Granted the first three assumptions, *any* departure from the allocation of resources that results from the natural and existing free play of the pricing mechanism constitutes a "distortion" or "misapplication" and hence "impedes" development, and government policy should be confined to insuring that distortions do not occur.

Probably Professor Johnson would not accept this bald summary of his assumptions. And yet, if we posit more realistic assumptions we may arrive at different conclusions. These assumptions are:

1) in most underdeveloped economies there exists a great mass of unemployed, mostly disguised. Since the Chicago School denies, by definition, that there is such a thing as disguised unemployment, I will change this statement, for its benefit, as follows: in most underdeveloped countries, the mobility mechanism is functioning so badly that a large portion of the work force is "engaged in work" of very low productivity affording scarcely more than a bare subsistence. In other words the existing allocation of the "work" force is very faulty in relation to conceivable alternatives;

2) the existing stock of capital equipment and natural resources are generally used with a very low degree of intensity;

3) the inequality of incomes is so great that the existing consumption-production pattern and the allocation of existing and new capital resources is "optimum" only in a very arbitrary sense of the term that has little real significance;

4) there is no presumption that government expenditures are more favorable to development than private expenditures;

5) there is widespread lack of confidence in the continuance of the democratic and free enterprise systems and non-pecuniary factors play an important role in investment decisions;

6) the industrial sector, both on the management and labor sides, is characterized by imperfect competition and the functioning of the pricing mechanism is affected accordingly;

7) in some underdeveloped economies, exports are dominated by one or two primary commodities produced under conditions of high absolute advantage.

Professor Johnson ignores or abstracts from most of these actual conditions. If he wishes to do a little exercise under arbitrary assumptions he has a perfect right to do so. But he should make clear to the reader what he is doing and should most certainly not pretend to be offering advice to actual policy makers without trying to ascertain and take account of actual conditions confronting those policy makers. Thus, in a country like Colombia, the *non*-use or misuse of factors of production, or the "distortions" in resource allocation resulting from gross inequality of income, may dwarf any hypothetical distortion resulting from the maintenance of a rate of exchange "too low" from the point of view of equilibrium in the balance of payments. Professor Johnson does not even limit his concept of equilibrium to current trade account but includes all invisible and presumably capital items. But a profound lack of underlying confidence may result in a chronic undervaluation of the local currency under conditions of a floating rate and freedom of capital movements.

If, owing to the peculiar structure of industry, organized labor and the import trade, a devaluation touches off a wave of "defensive" price and wage advances, its beneficent effect of bringing about an approach to parity in the external and internal value of a currency may be more than offset and the presumed decrease in pressure to import not materialize. The country then might suffer all the disruptive effects of devaluation with no offsetting benefits. It is not enough to reply that the internal price and wage structure *should* have risen by only three or four percent when actually it rose by twenty or thirty percent. An expert who presumes to offer advice on policy must take all conditions and possibilities into account.

In short, Professor Johnson has not proved his case for policy purposes by demonstrating that under *certain* conditions, a better allocation of resources may occur in the absence of measures to promote import-substitution *if in reality these conditions do not exist.* As Sidney Dell well puts it: "The problem [in an underdeveloped country] is then no longer one of allocating fixed resources to the most economic uses—as in a fully employed economy; rather it is one of finding productive employment for resources not otherwise used."[1]

Another consequence of the implicit assumption of full employment is that of unconsciously assuming that if import-substitution takes place, it must be at the expense of other production or of *exports*. In an economy in which there is a lot of slack, the impact of import-substitution on other domestic pro-

[1] Sidney Dell, *Trade Blocs and Common Markets* (London: Constable & Co., Ltd., 1963), p. 162.

duction and exports would require a demonstration for each country and each type of policy that Professor Johnson has failed to give. If it is retorted that this is an unreasonable requirement, I would remind the reader again that the author is offering general and unqualified advice to all underdeveloped countries and is not merely setting forth a hypothetical model that may possibly have relevance for policy makers. In other words, an import-substitution policy may result in a misallocation of resources or it may not. The matter cannot be settled by assuming constant full and efficient employment of resources, but by a consideration of likely alternative investment and employment under actual conditions in actual countries. One would have to present evidence, for example, that the quantitative restriction of vegetable oil and the consequent long term investment in African palm plantaciones in Colombia prejudiced in any way the export of raw cotton or of cattle that followed a specially favorable rate of exchange, or other production and employment for the domestic market. It is conceivable that it may have, but it cannot be proved by resort to a model resting on unrealistic assumptions.

Professor Johnson makes a further specific criticism of exchange rationing to the effect that in contrast to the use of a protective tariff, it confers windfall gains on importers who receive licenses or on consumers of their products and deprives the government of income that would be available for development purposes. Let us consider these three criticisms in order. I would concur in the first point on the grounds of the undesirability of adding to inequality of income. Professor Johnson is not concerned with this criticism, and it makes no difference to him if price markups are controlled so that the benefits are passed along to consumers. In both cases, the government is deprived of revenues otherwise available for "development." This is a curious position. Since the author subscribes to the full employment, more investment-more output point of view, the windfall profits might, in his view, be expected to add to saving, investment, output and hence "development." The "consumers" in this case are in the majority and, in the first instance, purchasers of intermediate and capital goods. If, through the device of rationing, the composition of imports is shifted to favor capital and intermediate goods, and their purchase and use are encouraged by what Professor Johnson would call an undervalued exchange rate, is not "development" also encouraged? There is no reason to assume that the government would make more efficient use of the money. Even if the benefits of the lower exchange rate and rationing are passed eventually along to bona fide consumers of goods domestically produced through the use of imported capital goods, is this necessarily bad in an economy where much slack prevails? It might be argued that the increased effective demand thus made possible hastens industrialization whereas additional funds received by an inefficient government may only result in waste. Clearly, the validity of Professor Johnson's point is not self-evident.

Here, as throughout, the author neglects the dynamic or interacting aspects. Under certain conditions, a rise of prices touched off by devaluation, or a rise in protective or revenue tariffs, may in turn endanger a precariously held stability in prices and thus bring in its train a whole series of disruptive developments.

Professor Johnson assumes that measures to encourage import substitution will be confined to facilities for final manufacturing processes. He quite rightly calls attention to the fact that some of such processes may be for "less essential" goods and have the unforeseen result of increasing the imports of raw materials and intermediate goods for their domestic production. The remedy (and the advice) in such cases would be, as Professor Johnson elsewhere suggests, a general tax on the consumption of non-essential goods. However, the misuse of a device, otherwise useful, does not justify its complete abandonment. Professor Johnson's disapproval is not limited to import substitutes of non-essential but of "essential" goods as well on the grounds of encouraging monopoly and of increasing the real cost to the economy of the goods in question and reducing "productivity." It is implied that protection characteristically fosters monopoly and inefficiency, so the new industries, instead of being a "dynamic" source of technical progress, will instead play "a parasitical role." The source of monopoly, a serious problem for reasons of cost-push inflation, not mentioned by Professor Johnson, are more often to be found in technological factors and the small internal market. However, to counter monopolistic tendencies by free trade may be a case of the cure being worse than the disease, especially as the cure may not touch monopolistic practices in labor. The solution may have to be sought in other measures. The high real cost and productivity argument depends again on the assumption of full employment.

It is perhaps natural but unjust to single out only the points in an argument with which one disagrees. Actually there is much of Professor Johnson's policy advice on which I am in agreement, such as matching the prohibition or high tariff on the import of luxury goods by a corresponding internal tax on consumption, though even here Professor Johnson would prefer a single tax on consumption or even better a well enforced progressive tax on income. One can sympathize with the latter view but at the same time point out that it took fifty years of political struggle and the help of two world wars and a long continued cold war to secure such a well enforced progressive tax in the developed countries, and, even so, the degree of inequality in buying power in the United States is still great.

Another good piece of advice is the danger of affording extravagant protection by permitting the free import of raw material and intermediate goods components. Certainly, the real degree of protection should be known and the danger of creating vested interests in the production of non-essential (and even essential) goods at an exorbitant cost should be stressed.

One can concede the dangers of exchange rationing and a policy of import substitution without necessarily going to the opposite course of free trade at a floating or "true equilibrium" rate of exchange. Let us for the moment consider the possible consequences of free trade and a free rate of exchange in one underdeveloped country (a) with a great advantage in the export of one primary product (b) but whose export of this product is limited by a world pact (as in the case of coffee) or by physical or other limitations (as in the case of petroleum). Although exchange may be generated very cheaply, the quantity is more or less fixed. With fortunes earned by importers and relatively high incomes by coffee growers or petroleum workers, the demand for imports of consumer goods, foreign travel and study, and export of capital, may exhaust the available supplies of exchange for many years. The governments will probably place high priority on public health so that the population increases rapidly. With limited employment opportunities in coffee growing and petroleum, more and more people will remain in subsistence type agriculture. Transport protection may permit some local industries. The amount of "exchange protection" will depend on the strength of consumer demand, which will be strongly influenced by the degree of inequality of income. The greater the inequality, the higher the "natural" rate of exchange is likely to be and hence the greater the "protection" to the manufacture of articles of mass consumption, such as beer, and to the production of certain articles demanded by the well-to-do outside the subsistence sector. It hardly appears to be a condition favoring rapid development. An equilibrium rate strongly influenced by inequality of income has little claim to be exalted as an optimum rate in any significant sense of the term.

Professor Johnson tacitly assumes that an equilibrium rate is somehow a "good" rate. If however the equilibrium is one that equates limited exports with imports of luxury type consumer goods and export of capital, there is little to be said for it. Before issuing a blanket endorsement of a classical free trade model, it behooves economists to study very closely their assumptions, and especially the implicit assumptions in relation to the actual conditions applicable to each country. If, for example, the conditions are so different from those that confronted currently developed countries in their earlier stages and are such as to raise grave doubts about whether the free enterprise system, even with the removal of restraints and controls, can reasonably be expected to permit the "minimum critical effort" to break through "the low income equilibrium trap" (Harvey Leibenstein's phrase), then the free trade approach and the equilibrating of the foreign balance through a floating exchange rate will effectively tie the hands of any progressive or reform government intent on accelerating development. True, the equilibrium rate may rise so high as to give protection all around. But the cumulative and spiral effect on the domestic price and income structure may be so in excess of the anticipated "arithmetical" effect as to wreck or discredit the domestic program. And even so, the windfall import profits may lead to a diversion of exchange for imported luxury goods. Following two devaluations and a rise of customs tariffs to 230 percent and even 330 percent, the import of private automobiles was permitted in Colombia. This resulted in a substantial volume of purchases representing not only an immediate wasteful use of extremely limited exchange resources but a continued diversion of exchange and domestic savings in the future. To retort that Colombia should tackle the basic problem of inequality of incomes doubtless salves one's conscience but hardly is an answer to an immediate problem.

While I have been rather critical of Professor Johnson's advice, this does not imply a blanket approval of actual policies in this field. There are, fortunately, a variety of alternatives. In the specific case of Colombia, in the actual conditions in which it finds itself, the following policies in this general field appear appropriate:

(1) *The dominant export.* A special relatively low rate applicable to coffee exports. Colombia is a member of the World Coffee Pact under which it undertakes to limit its exports. Its advantages for coffee growing are so great that a relatively low rate is sufficient to provide the exports permitted. A higher rate encourages a long term increase in supplies, which would lead to serious problems of financing retained stocks or, in other words, a misallocation of resources. This relatively low rate, however, would make imports excessively cheap and would make

most manufactures and the growing of many foodstuffs impossible without high protection.

(2) *The treatment of most imports.* In this field, therefore, the choice must be between a higher rate of exchange, import licensing or rationing, high protective and revenues tariffs, or a combination of these measures.

The preference (or prejudice?) of most economists of developed countries would probably be for a sufficiently high rate of exchange to permit equilibrium in the balance of payment without resort to licensing or rationing. As a second line of defense they would accept a revenue tariff on imported consumers goods and would recommend that it apply also to the same goods domestically produced. In order of preference they would then accept a protective tariff, provided the true degree of protection is known, is not too excessive, and is applied to industries which can look forward to internal and/or external economies.

Few would accept, even in third place, import licensing or rationing, usually because of arbitrariness in administration, windfall profits to a few fortunate importers, the excessive temptation to resort to bribery, and, in the case of prohibited goods, danger of excessive "protection" to non-essential products and consequent misallocation of resources. These are weighty objections. They can only be answered, as in the analogous resort to rationing in wartime, by the existence of overriding considerations of the highest urgency. Few economists, curiously enough, will concede the existence of such overriding considerations in the case of development and yet the necessity of development would appear to be as important as that of most wars.

The difficulty of rationing, as commonly practiced, lies in the lack of appropriate criteria. Officials have been free to indulge their prejudices. At one moment, the criterion may be to foster competition; at another, to avoid excess capacity. The distinction between essential and non-essential imports may be extremely arbitrary. Or luxury imports may be permitted because otherwise they will become contraband, with its evils and loss of revenue to the government. Or the criterion may be import-substitution with future saving of foreign exchange. Once a factory is established, perhaps with foreign capital, the pressure is strong to permit import of raw materials and intermediate goods to provide employment, no matter how luxurious the good may be or how low the employment-investment ratio may be. At one moment the criterion may be employment; at another, productivity. And so on. Under these conditions, it is not surprising that licensing as practiced is open to many valid criticisms.

On the other hand, in the absence of rationing, the problem of flight capital, so serious in many underdeveloped countries that combine great inequality of incomes with a growing lack of confidence in the future, is difficult to handle. Generalized and chronic undervaluation of the currency may not only not check a steady flight of capital for security reasons and the import of luxury goods, but make the cost of capital imports far in excess of its "shadow" price. Moreover the gyrations in the rate may not be conducive either to confidence or domestic price stability. The diversity and inconsistency of criteria for licensing may apply with equal force to tariff policies. Governmental revenues derived from tariffs may not only encourage extravagance and waste (the lack of soundly based criteria apply equally to government expenditures) but their final incidence may be regressive and discourage reforms in the application of progressiveness in taxation.

Is there any way out of these difficulties? This depends, it would seem, on the nature of the plan of development and the dedication with which it is implemented. If, for example, the immediate goal of a national plan is a rise in the economic and educational levels of the lowest half of the population, and it appears that this necessitates the creation of X number of jobs outside of agriculture in X years, and this in turn indicates a concentration of effort in the wage goods comprised in the worker's cost-of-living index, and this in turn suggests the need of a marked rise in the employment-capital ratio of existing and newly imported capital and the restriction on the growth in demand for goods and services not in the workers' cost of living index (or not for the production of such goods and services), we would begin to have rational criteria for both the application of protection and import licensing as arms of the national plan.

In this case, the hypothetical "under" or "over" valuations of the external value of the national currency need not have the distortion effects on the allocation of resources feared by Professor Johnson, and we could avoid some of the more serious distortion effects of great inequality of incomes and capital flight.

(3) *The treatment of exports.* The main disadvantage of avoiding frequent changes in the principal import rate is that of worsening the position of exports other than the dominant one in which the country may possess a great advantage. This, theoretically, could be avoided by an export subsidy that compensates for a rise in domestic costs. Subsidies, however, are difficult to administer and invite retaliation. A more feasible course would be the creation of a rate of exchange that, while not exactly floating, would be subject to adjustment in acordance with the movement of an index which is judged to be a tolerable reflection of changes in domestic costs. The base year could be one in which it appears that a number of goods were exported without excessive losses or gains. In Colombia, for a number of years, we have suffered from alternating periods of overvaluation and undervaluation of exchange for export purposes which have resulted in alternating periods of losses with restriction of exports, and windfall profits and expansion of exports. The results have been disruptive to both the internal and external markets and have militated against efficient development of new exports.

Such an arrangement can be defended against the charge of dumping as it is explicitly limited to compensating for a rise in costs. It is not a subsidy as much as a compensation for growing obstacles to exports.

This same rate of exchange might also be used for certain imports and the payment of certain services that do not affect the general price structure, such as basic allotments of exchange for travel abroad, for foreign educational or medical expenses, for approved remittances of dividends and salary payments and so forth. This course would have the incidental advantage of avoiding making the central bank absorb exchange losses by buying dollars from exporters at one rate of exchange and selling them at a lower rate to importers.

Withholding of exports to obtain a higher rate of exchange might take place in short periods, but generally goods are either perishable or entail heavy costs for storage, and exporters need a steady flow of funds to meet current costs. It is not believed, therefore, that this danger is too serious or cannot be met.

(4) *The free rate.* The use of different exchange rates for different exports, imports and specified services necessarily implies a market for certain transactions not covered by the other markets. These would include on the side of the offer of foreign currencies, the "unregistered" import of capital, foreign tourists' expenditures, the proceeds of contraband exports and, on the demand side, the export of capital, tourist expenditures abroad of nationals, payments in excess of those allotted by the "minor exports rate," and payment for contraband imports. The objective would be to dry up as much as possible the offer of dollars in this market so that as little capital as possible could be exported as well as payments abroad that offer little aid to the development plan. For this and other reasons, it would be preferable not to make it a legal rate so that transactions in this market could not be legally enforced, and to provide reasonable facilities for certain types of payment at the minor export market rate. Not being a legal rate, it could be arranged that it not be published and it would not be the highest legal rate for conversion purposes for P.L. 480 purchase of American surplus agricultural goods. While not legal, it might be preferable not to make it illegal except for lack of enforcibility of contracts and lack of quotation in the press.

In summary, for the conditions prevailing in Colombia and assuming the existence and implementation of a rational and defensible overall plan of development, at least three legal rates and one illegal (or better one non-legally enforceable rate) of exchange could be defended. The major export and import rates could be subject to periodic readjustment, depending on the course of internal prices. The minor export and miscellaneous payments rate could be subject to more frequent and automatic adjustment in accordance with the rise of an index of representative costs. Dollars would be rationed or allotted in accordance with the priorities of the overall plan of development. To minimize the dangers stressed by Professor Johnson, tariffs on or rationing of finished goods—the production or consumption of which it is desired to discourage—should be supplemented by appropriate restrictions on raw materials and intermediate goods and by excise taxes.

Economists of the classical free trade persuasion may feel that all this smacks of gadgetry. In reply I would point out that even developed countries with thousands of items entering into their balances of payments and with perfect confidence in their long term futures have on occasion thought it necessary to maintain a non-equilibrium rate by resort not only to monetary policy but also to a variety of direct and indirect measures. As of the date of writing both England and the United States have resorted to an abundance of such measures. In wartime, of course, rationing is the rule rather than the exception. Is not the achievement of a breakthrough in development as important as a war and justifies as great a concentration of effort?

Professor Johnson concludes with a short section on foreign investment. Here he abandons his previous assumption of full employment and implicitly assumes that any and every foreign investment adds to national income by not only the value added by the foreign owned capital but also by the value added by all the other factors plus taxes and plus the resulting external economies of scale. At this point Professor Johnson emulates the cuttle fish and takes refuge behind an ink cloud so that I am not sure I fully grasp his point. "Foreign private investment in a country . . . raises its national income by the value at market prices of the marginal product of the capital and the increase in value at market prices of the marginal products of the domestic factors it employs, whereas the foreign investor receives the value of the marginal product of this capital at factor cost (not of indirect taxes) less the direct taxes he has to pay to the country's government (corporate income tax, non-resident withholding tax)." Since the foreign investor presumably receives the going (high) rate of return on capital and the indirect and corporate taxes are generally considered to be passed along to the consumer, I do not think we need be unduly exercised over the difference between his gross and net return. Here, it will be noted, foreign investment is assumed to increase employment and earnings of other factors, which assumes a high degree of slack (disguised unemployment?). It is concluded "Cases in which a country loses by foreign investment in it are extremely difficult to construct." Possible domestic monopoly by a foreign firm as a result of import-substitution now becomes "within the control of domestic economic policy." This abrupt turnaround tempts one to remark "don't look now, but your bias is showing." Suppose an oil company secures its oil on ridiculously low terms? Suppose, after a small initial investment, the foreign company finances its expansion by borrowing in the local market from banks or from so called "Cooley Loans" (up to 25% of the proceeds of P.L. 480 loans) so that remittances amount to many times the original investment? Suppose that the local company shows no profit, but that the profits appear in the foreign parent company's account in the sale of equipment, licensing fees, fees for technical assistance, and so forth? Or suppose a foreign investment creates a vested interest for the production of a luxury good that is not only unnecessary but entails heavy social cost, such as the assembly of private automobiles in a very poor country? Surely it is not so extremely difficult to construct cases in which a country loses by foreign investment even without taking advantage of Professor Johnson's previous assumption that there is no slack in the system so that the production of one good must be at the expense of another. On this assumption the loss in value added and taxes must be subtracted from the new values added plus the new taxes paid.

Here, as in other cases, generalized statements do not help us very much in matters of policy formulation. Foreign investment, like domestic, must be considered case by case, or at least category by category, and in relation to the overall plan of development. In certain cases, great benefits have resulted from such investment; in others, the benefits have been extremely dubious. In still others, they may be on balance advantageous, but could be even more so. Models and equilibrium analysis cannot take us very far in this difficult policy field.

IX

Mobility, Employment and Output: Interacting Elements in a Theory of Development*

Various writers have pointed out the beneficial effect on the growth of gross national product by a shift of workers from lower to higher paid occupations, and this shift or mobility[1] has been noted as part of the explanation of the rapid rates of growth experienced by various European countries and by Japan in the fifties and early sixties. It was also noted in the Basis of a Development Program for Colombia, edited by Lauchlin Currie, International Bank for Reconstruction, 1951.[2] Much later, in developing what I called the breakthrough approach to the problem of accelerating development,[3] I sought to convert this

* I am indebted to V. Lewis Bassie for most helpful comments on a first draft of this note.

[1] I mean by mobility not movement but the ability to shift from lower to higher paying jobs.

[2] Lauchlin Currie (ed.), Basis of a Development Program for Colombia, International Bank for Reconstruction, 1951, pp. 28-29.

[3] Lauchlin Currie, *Accelerating Development: The Necessity and the Means* (New York: The McGraw-Hill Book Co., 1966), pp. 84-114.

observed experience into an important element of a deliberate and planned program of development for a certain group of underdeveloped countries. My interest was not so much in achieving a more rapid rate of growth in the G.N.P. per capita, as in achieving "the critical minimum effort" to overcome "the low-income equilibrium"[4] and bring about a fall in the birth rate as a necessary condition for underdeveloped countries to gain greater control over their environment.

The subject has generally been treated as an interesting but rather exceptional case. It seems to me to be sufficiently common and important to deserve more attention in the literature of growth and development. For this purpose, however, it requires a more generalized statement than I gave it in my book. There I was concerned with the possibility of reducing the army of disguised unemployed by creating more job opportunities outside of agriculture. These disguised unemployed are largely agriculturalists with very low productivity whose output could be replaced rather easily by an extension of commercial type farming and by the consolidation of uneconomic-sized holdings. I assumed that the addition to the production of non-agricultural goods and services would not so lower the prices of those products, and the (temporarily) lost agricultural production would not so raise agricultural prices and incomes, as to leave the deflated G.N.P. per capita unchanged. Failure to examine this assumption more closely was perhaps not a serious lapse in the case with which I was dealing. For a more generalized statement, however, the implications of the assumption need to be explicitly stated.

We may generalize, therefore, that a shift of workers from lower paying occupations (A) to higher paying occupations (B), or a relative growth in the numbers of workers in the latter, will not only tend to bring about a greater equality of incomes but will also increase real incomes per capita when a larger proportion of the additional income is spent on the output of B than

[4] Harvey Leibenstein, *Economic Backwardness and Economic Growth* (New York: John Wiley & Sons, 1957), Chapters 8, 10.

on the output of A. This will be the case where the income elasticity of demand for the products of B is greater than for the products of A. This in turn implies that the relation of price elasticity of demand and supply elasticity for products of A do not result in a greater proportion of income being spent on them than previously. If this assumption does not hold, and a shift occurs, incomes in A would rise relatively to B and presumably the shift of workers would be discouraged or even reversed. In general this would be a rather exceptional case. It would occur only when the shift brought about a continuing reduction in supply in the face of a sharp rise in price resulting from a marked price inelasticity of demand. More customary appears to be the case where a shift from A to B leaves the higher average earnings in B little affected but results in a gradual rise in average earnings in A, restrained by high elasticity of supply (as in agriculture in developed countries) or by such alternatives as labor saving devices in place of manual workers or domestic servants. The very fact that a shift is occurring is usually a reflection of a long continued "over-supply" and "over-production" (in relative terms) in the occupation from which migration is occurring, or in which the relative proportion of the working force is declining. It may be objected that increased employment in higher paying activities automatically means higher per capita income and no further explanation is necessary. However, it seems worthwhile to bring out the implicit assumptions on which such an "obvious" result rests.

We have here, I believe, a principle of considerable importance for the reason that when the mobility mechanism is functioning reasonably well, there is a constant and considerable movement from the production of goods and services for the demand of which there is less income elasticity of demand to the production of things for which there is a greater elasticity. Thus the additional production resulting from the shift in employment does not result in an offsetting fall in price and total value of output. What happens to the price and value of production of (A) depends on the growth of productivity and/or the elasticity of supply, in relation to the relatively low increase in demand as incomes in the other sectors rise. The relative shift of workers out of agriculture in developed countries was a factor tending to compensate for the relatively high elasticity of supply resulting in turn from growth in physical productivity.[5] On the other hand, the attraction of workers out of domestic service by higher wages and consequent rise in the price of such services encountered a relatively low elasticity of supply of such services. The strong demand for domestic services was therefore diverted to all the gadgets and expedients and changes in patterns of consumption that constitute the well known response to a "shortage" of domestic help.

If the mobility mechanism is not functioning well, as happens in many underdeveloped countries, there may be a perverse movement to the lowest paying occupations, e.g. agriculture, or what might be called inverse mobility. In this case the elasticity factors may not only bring about a perverse change in the distribution of income but an absolute decline per capita. This could follow from an increase in subsistence type farming (disguised unemployed) while commercial type farming was expanding. It is an advantage of the concept of disguised unemployment that it enables us more easily to grasp the consequence of a faulty working of mobility.

Although, as I mentioned at the beginning, various writers have pointed out in specific cases the implications for rapid growth of a pool of low-wage labor to draw on, it does not appear that the full implication of mobility has been sufficiently exploited. For example, with the recent tendency to displace investment or capital formation as the main factor in the explanation of the growth of output, there has been a good deal of speculation on the nature of "technological progress," with attempts to break it down in its component elements. Is it not possible

[5] Professor Evsey Domar in a private communication quite correctly pointed out that while the elasticity of supply of agricultural goods is generally high in certain cases it may be low. The implication is that a shift of any size out of agriculture will not always and invariably raise per capita income.

that the greatly improved mobility in the United States, as shown by the tendency of incomes from work to become more equal, is itself an important element in "technical progress" or the growth in output unaccountable by the increase in investment? By the same token, when substantial equality of earnings is achieved, will it not be more difficult to maintain the same rate of growth in the value of output?

E. F. Dennison considered the possible contribution to output per capita resulting from a shift from lower to higher paying occupations and dismissed it as negligible (0.05 percentage points of the growth rate in the United States from 1929 to 1957).[6] He reached this surprising conclusion by making adjustments for the "quality" of labor (as measured by years of education). "Adjusted" in this way, earnings per person employed in farming were eighty-six percent as high as those in nonfarm activities in 1954.[7] Such an adjustment, however, appears to be completely uncalled for, since it reflects one aspect of a social situation in which opportunities open to city dwellers have been better. "Years of education" have little if any direct economic significance and the concept is as unmanageable as was Keynes' wage units. Widespread technical education may increase the output of the *total* working force. Differences in education, however, cannot be invoked to account for differences in earnings as between groups except as they operate to limit the supply of work in a group, or, in other words, as a factor impeding mobility. Dropping this "adjustment" for quality of the labor and treating the effect of education (or its lack) under the factors increasing or decreasing mobility would appear to be the more defensible course.

This conclusion has obvious implications for the various attempts to measure the economic value of education with reference to particular groups. The value attributed to "education" is more properly attributed to the ability education confers to

6 E. F. Dennison, Sources of Economic Growth in the United States, Committee of Economic Development, N. Y., 1962, p. 227.

7 *Ibid.*, p. 227.

enter a better paying occupation. With perfect mobility it is conceivable that many of the occupations requiring the highest educational standards would be the lowest paying, because of the agreeable nature of the work and the fact that education is increasingly not regarded as a cost in the sense of being a deterrent to entering professions. This does not mean that education has no influence on national productivity per capita. It would appear very difficult however, and of dubious utility, to attempt to disentangle its effect in this context from the other items comprised in technological progress.

Another reason why Dennison was led to minimize the contribution to output per capita resulting from better mobility, or a better allocation of the working force, is that he attributed the major part of the effect arising from mobility to the relative growth of components of the gross product in which the advance in productivity has been exceptionally fast. Thus he states, quite correctly, that "If there is a shift of resources from low-paying to high-paying industries, the total measured real national output will rise even if output per unit of input in each separate industry is unchanged and there is no change in the resources used in the economy as a whole."[8] But by the use of the broad term "resources" and attributing the growth in output to "industry shifts" again he was led to minimize the importance of the mobility of labor in accounting for changes in output per capita.

Some writers have come dangerously close to treating of the growth in expenditures on services in the higher income countries as a disadvantage because the physical productivity in such fields is alleged to be lower than in agriculture or manufacturing. Indeed, this appears to be the theoretical base of the action of the British Government in levying a payroll tax on service industries. However, in the light of the argument of this note, any attempt to create inverse mobility, i.e. shifts from higher to lower paying activities, may only decrease the value of output per capita. The benefits of high physical productivity in agriculture and manufacturing are shown not so much in the in-

[8] *Ibid.*, p. 225.

creased value of output of those fields but rather in the release of manpower to meet the new demands and in the production of which higher incomes can be made. There appears to be a widespread feeling that greater technological progress is possible in the production of things than in services. This, however, is not certain and in any case is relative. All the scientists and technicians who participated in the development of computers and devices to further automation not only made it possible to do things that could not be done before but, over time, have released and will release large numbers of people for the performance of other services. At least some of the technical advances in services have outshone those in the production of hard goods.

There has been some speculation on the explanation of the relative shares of income accruing to owners and to workers. Bowley thought he had found here a relationship of significant constancy, but more recently, at least up to 1963-64, the proportion accruing to work appears to have been rising. Since greater mobility increases the value of output per capita and since the shifts are likely to be to service industries where the proportion of gross output attributable to labor is usually higher, is it not possible that better mobility may be part of the explanation of the overall rising share attributable to work, when such a rise occurs?[9]

The interposition of imperfect competition in industry and in labor may impede mobility, perpetuate marked differences in earnings and thus impede the growth in the value of output per capita. Or we may generalize by saying that whatever factor impedes mobility, or a better distribution of the work force as measured by a greater equality of earnings brought about by a relative movement of workers from lower to higher paying work, by the same token impedes the rate of growth in per capita out-

[9] V. Lewis Bassie warned in 1958 that there were no good grounds for expecting either constancy in the relation of work to property income or an indefinite continuance of shifts in one direction or another. The apparent rise in the relative share of property incomes in 1964-66 gives point to his warning. *Economic Forecasting* (New York: The McGraw-Hill Book Co., 1958), p. 429. The discussion above refers to a possible explanation of a shift favoring the share of labor.

put. It should be noted that it is not the greater equality of earnings that in itself brings about a rise in per capita income but only that greater equality which results from the relative growth in numbers in the better paying jobs, that is, the greater equality that results from levelling up rather than levelling down.

Insofar as the Abolition of Poverty Program is successful in promoting a better distribution of the work force, it will yield continuing dividends in higher average income or output in the future.

Finally, by focusing on the benefits to be derived from better mobility, a much more promising approach to the problem of underdevelopment becomes available than by focusing on improving "productivity" of all workers where they are and in what they are doing. Similarly, the dangers of perverse mobility can more easily be grasped. We are prone to fall victims to the tendency to define concepts in water-tight compartments, forgetting that "nature makes no abrupt transitions." So with such concepts as unemployment, disguised unemployment, underemployment, mobility and the distribution of the work force. Increases in output resulting from greater employment or less disguised or under-employment, and from greater mobility or a "better" distribution of the work force, are actually closely related. The effect on output of greater employment may be offset by poorer mobility or by an increase in under-employment. Greater mobility may permit a rise in G.N.P. per capita despite increased unemployment. It would appear worthwhile to treat these various aspects of employment together. Even greater "productivity" may only be the consequence of better mobility.

Does it follow that the attainment of a substantial degree of equality of income is a "handicap" because the stimulus to the rate of growth resulting from the process of attaining greater equality disappears? To take this position, it seems to me, is to confuse means to an end with the end itself. The rate of growth in the value of output per capita at constant prices should be more a means to an end than an end in itself. A tendency toward greater equality of income in nonsocialist developed countries, would be accompanied by a relatively high income per capita. In other words, the material benefits of a rapid growth in the value of output have already, in very large part, been attained in economically advanced societies. A slower rate of growth in this particular series may be indicated in order, in Professor Galbraith's happy phrase, to enhance the quality of living, which, rationally considered, is a better end than is an indefinite increase in production of material things. A good case can be made for the contention that the greater the mobility of labor and the higher the average income with such mobility, the slower should be the growth in the G.N.P. per capita both because of the lower opportunities for further mobility and the substitution of leisure, education and so forth for hard goods. The poorer the distribution of the working force and the lower the incomes of the great majority of the people, as in most underdeveloped countries, the higher should be (though unfortunately not necessarily will be) the growth in output per capita.

In conclusion, the attainment of greater mobility, or a better distribution of the work force, appears to have played a more important role in the development of economically advanced societies, and is worthy of much more attention in resolving the problem of underdevelopment than it has been accorded in the literature.

X

Why Foreign Aid?

I do not know whether a provocative and penetrating article by Professor Hans Morgenthau on a Political Theory of Foreign Aid[1] has been widely read and commented upon. It certainly deserves to be for the important issues it raises and the challenging positions it takes on what is perhaps the major problem of our time.

He distinguishes aid for some six different purposes—humanitarian, subsistence, military, bribery, prestige and economic development. I am not here concerned with the first five motivations and their justification. It is in the discussion of aid for economic development that the most difficult and controversial issues are raised. Professor Morgenthau is quite frankly skeptical both of the possibilities of success of this type of aid in achieving its avowed purpose and whether it actually serves the interests of the giving nation.

In connection with the probable degree of success he points out that the implicit assumption that development is merely

1 Reprinted in David Novack and Robert Lekachman, *Development and Society* (New York: St. Martin's Press, 1963), from "Why Foreign Aid?" Robert Goldwin (ed.) by the Public Affairs Conference Center, University of Chicago, 1963.

129

a matter of the infusion of capital and technical knowledge is not well founded in fact and that the spectacular success of the Marshall Plan has tended to make us overlook the very different circumstances and conditions underlying the Marshall Plan and the current typical aid programs. He could have made his case even stronger by pointing out that scarcely any recipient countries have made the transition from the underdeveloped to the developed category or to the category where the rate of population growth has fallen to a point where it can be said that the country is in assured control of its economic environment. Invoking the criteria of the degree of mass and growing poverty and of viable functioning the record to date is one of grim failure.

On his second main point, whether aid for economic development, even if attended with some success, will serve the interest of the giving country, Professor Morgenthau questions the assumed correlations between social stability and democratic institutions, and between democratic institutions and a peaceful foreign policy, citing examples and hypothetical cases that cast doubts on such correlations.

His conclusion naturally follows that a policy of foreign aid is no different from diplomatic or military policy or propaganda. They are all weapons in the political armory of a nation. It follows, therefore, that the case for each type of aid must be judged on its merits and it is the political expert whose voice must carry the final word. "The problem of foreign aid is insoluble if it is considered as a self-sufficient technical enterprise of a primarily economic nature."

Professor Morgenthau makes out a strong case and yet, if there is no escape from his conclusion, one is left with feelings of dismay. Consider, for a moment, the possibilities. In many of the most densely populated countries, population is already pressing on resources and they are becoming more and more dependent on gifts or purchases of food. Exports of food from North America have increased enormously in the past thirty years and it is now the only truly large scale source of such exports. Exports in 1965-66 reached the almost incredible figure of sixty million tons.

Parallel with this growing dependency is the growing indebtedness. Most "aid" is in the form of loans. Consequently all underdeveloped non-Communist countries are going deeper in debt to the developed (overwhelmingly, in the final analysis, the United States) and are becoming increasingly dependent on this continuing process. The AID estimates that a continuance of present rates would mean a debt of ninety billion dollars by 1975. The servicing of the existing debt now amounts to thirty percent of the new aid extended annually and this percentage may be expected to rise steadily. This means that a cessation of new loaning or *even a slackening* plunges the heavily indebted underdeveloped countries into grave exchange difficulties. The alternatives are repudiation which, unless carried out with the consent of the lending countries and called "refinancing," means no more aid, or an acceptance of whatever conditions that may be laid down by the lenders.

There is nothing more hazardous than forecasting and yet we have to take such hazards in projecting current trends. If the recent trends in the Communist countries to limit the rate of population growth are continued it is probable that their dependence on food imports will pass and may even be replaced by an export capability. If, however, current population trends continue in underdeveloped countries in Latin America, Africa, the Middle East and S.E. Asia, their dependence on outside aid, for one group of countries or another, will probably grow.

So we come back to Professor Morgenthau's conclusion. The developed countries, and especially the United States, are already and will be increasingly in a position to intervene in the policies of the underdeveloped countries, and to lay down conditions for continued aid which will be difficult for them not to accept. This places a tremendous responsibility on the United States especially if the use of aid is not to be for economic development but as an arm of political and foreign policy. The existence of American political experts in a hundred or so countries, who vary aid and the conditions for aid to accord with the presumed current interest of the United States in each country, is not a reassuring prospect. The one avenue of escape a currently underdeveloped country would have from extreme dependence on foreign powers would be to succeed in economic development, i.e. put itself in a position to control its own economic environment, and this possibility would be gravely weakened if the extension of aid is to be determined by political and foreign policy considerations rather than economic, and economists are to remain subordinated to diplomats.

Despite the dismal record to date, Professor Morgenthau is undoubtedly right when he says that most Americans believe that development is taking place and despite all obstacles and setbacks, is inevitable. This view rests on the natural tendency to believe that all or almost all countries are following in the footsteps of the advanced countries and the view is reinforced by the publication of statistics showing a greater growth in gross national product than of population, and by the visual confirmation afforded by swarming cities, high buildings, traffic congestions and great dams, steel plants and so on. It is only when we take into account the frightening increase in the number of very poor people, the rise in the rate of population growth so that in many countries the population is now doubling every twenty-three years, the increasingly unfavorable relation of dependents to workers, and of workers to natural resources, and the sharply rising cost of public services in rapidly growing cities, and various other indices, does the suspicion arise that in a more profound sense of the term there has been no development and the problem of underdevelopment is growing more acute. Since practically all underdeveloped countries are characterized by extreme inequality of income, the condition of the masses, whose numbers are continually growing, may actually have worsened. For example, Colombia, from 1951 to 1964, experienced technical revolutions in agriculture and transport comparable to the opening of the Midwest in the United States in the past century. The result, however, was not a marked rise in the general standard of living, but the ability to support fifty percent more people at continued low levels, with higher incomes for perhaps twenty to thirty percent of the people—the propertied classes, the relatively small middle class and the organized urban workers. Whether or not this constitutes development depends on what definition we care to use.

Regardless of definitions, a continuation of the trends of the past two decades would mean that a part of the world would be enjoying a standard of living so high that many objects of expenditure would appear incredibly frivolous to the rest of the world, the bulk of whose people would not as yet have been able to emerge from the "pain economy" stage. The relative percentages of people in the two worlds would depend on what occurs in China, but in any case would be weighted heavily on the side of the poor. In short, it seems probable that a continuation of present trends must result in a horrible degree of inequality on an international scale and an extreme degree of dependence of the poor nations on the rich for charity in order to live or to avoid a deterioration in already low standards. It is, of course, always possible that present trends may suddenly change, but to rely on this happening could only be a gamble.

The question then becomes, would such a world be in the best interests of the developed countries and particularly of the United States? From the standpoint of Dr. Morgenthau's argument, the answer would probably have to be in the affirmative. The dependence for food, new loans and gifts would be so great that the "political officers" could have a field day manipulating the course of events in a good part of the world. But would this really be the kind of world the United States would care to live in—a world of intense poverty for the majority of people, envy, frustration and resentment bordering on hatred of their benefactors and manipulators, and highly unstable in its internal composition? For one thing, much more stringent precautions to prevent an ever-growing influx of people from the underdeveloped parts of the world would have to be taken by the developed countries. For another, such a world could only breed violence and political overturns. The probability of mass killing and even starvation would not be the deterrent to such upheavals that might be expected since the new men struggling for power could always blame such conditions on the stoppage of aid. Moreover, poor as the poor countries may be, they can all, sooner or later, come into possession of the equipment necessary for nuclear warfare. It is said that India could to-day develop this in eighteen months. Would it be part of American policy first to shut off aid and then to occupy any country where it feels its interests are threatened? This could, at least in theory, lead to an occupation of much of the world.

But what, then, are the alternatives? Putting aside for the moment the question of how it might be accomplished, would the widespread attainment of a decent minimum standard of well-being (or absence of ill-being) in the greater part of the world and, of still greater importance, the assurance that such standards could be indefinitely maintained and even raised without foreign aid be for or against the American interest? It would, it is true, greatly lessen the dependence on the developed countries and hence the opportunities of manipulation through economic pressures on their part. On the other hand, any widespread developments that would create a less congenial atmosphere for the growth of envy, frustration, fear and hate are surely in the broader, longer term interests of the developed peoples, and especially the United States. Professor Morgenthau spoke of the spectacular success of the Marshall Plan (of which the great part, incidentally, was a gift) in its economic and political aspects. Might not an equally successful economic program for, say, Latin America, be expected to be followed by lessened tensions and at least the creation of conditions more propitious for peaceful co-existence than will otherwise exist?

Guarantees, in a matter of this sort, cannot be given. Individual backslidings to dictatorships, to local threats of war, to repudiation of debts or hostile treatment of foreign capital may be expected to occur but should not be allowed to divert us from the main chance and from playing the probabilities. The important thing, it seems to me, is not country by country manipulation to attain short term objectives, but the development of a successful formula or formulae for the attainment of viable development that can be more or less generally applied. If this can be done, it means that more people in what are now underdeveloped countries will be studying and thinking and hence less susceptible to violent emotional appeals (I only say *less*). These are the conditions that in time can be expected to unseat dictators and at least to allow the thin small voice of reason to be raised and heard.

With the change in the character of weapons, the United States must look for its ultimate security to a more peace loving and more rational world, less dominated by the destructive emotions —a world in which identity of interests can be demonstrated. Such identity cannot be established today and cannot be established as long as much of the world has no purposeful control over its environment and is dependent on charity or on loans it cannot repay.

Regarding foreign aid as an instrument of foreign policy in a narrow sense is only one of the obstacles to a re-orientation of policy more in harmony with the deeper and long-term interests of the United States. Other obstacles are the very natural but basically irrelevant humanitarian motivations and the expectation of gratitude. The proper analogy, here, it seems to me, can be found within the United States in the contrast between the old fashioned attitude toward the poor, the demoralized and the delinquent and the newer, detached and more scientific attitude. The old attitude was compounded of charity, exhortation and punishment. The danger to society of a demoralized and rebellious element is now better recognized, together with the extreme difficulty of the job of rehabilitation and the conversion of such elements into viable, properly functioning units of society. In many cases, success may only ultimately be achieved with the children. Expectations of gratitude are irrelevant, and failures in individual cases must be expected.

Applying this analogy to the question at issue, I would urge that little weight be accorded the current political attitudes of current governments of underdeveloped countries or to whether such governments are properly grateful or friendly. Just as in the case of an individual the important thing is rehabilitation or the attainment of the ability to be self-supporting, so in the case of aid for economic development the important thing is success in economic development. Success will be accompanied by a growth in the basic conditions that favor the longer term interests of the United States. Without success, no amount of manipulation or gratitude will create enduring conditions favorable to a peaceful world.

It may be noted that the same argument I have been developing on an international scale can be used within many of the underdeveloped countries themselves. The relatively small well-to-do and educated class can choose to lead and control the necessary economic and social transformations to make development in their countries a reality rather than a myth, which would imply a willingness to accept a smaller percentage of a rapidly growing pie, or they can place their faith in the police and the army and try to get an even larger slice of a small pie. Can it be doubted that, over the longer term, the true interest of this class is to create a society of diffused well-being, with an identity of interests and a stationary or slowly growing population? Unfortunately the only precedents for such an enlightened attitude are in countries with very different cultural inheritances. What is badly needed to enlist the cooperation of currently governing groups is a demonstration whose applicability they will accept.

It is not difficult to establish the case that *to date*, technology has been more of a curse than a blessing to mankind—in just the past two decades it has resulted in a billion or so more people living on the margin of subsistence, and in much greater and conspicuous inequality in the underdeveloped world and as between nations. It can also be argued that a relatively small and misconceived program of foreign aid may not only be unsuccessful, but by its very existence may block alternative approaches of greater promise and enable all underdeveloped countries to encroach more and more on their natural resources and thus make the chances of eventual catastrophic failure on a much greater scale more probable. To treat a continuing infection by a small but continuous treatment of antibiotics may only end by the patient becoming steadily weaker and a virus developing resistant to further injections—in short, in a much worse state than before the treatment began. To my mind, the main criticism of the aid program today should be directed at its lack of success in promoting viable economies whose development has become assured and self-generating.

But to attain success in development, are not conditions necessary, and will not these conditions be resented and resisted? Conditions are certainly necessary and it is quite possible that they may be resented. Much depends on the nature and appropriateness of the conditions, on who imposes them and how it is done, and whether the conditions actually accomplish the objective of enabling an economy to pass from the underdeveloped to the developed category. Conditions imposed by international lending agencies may be resented or criticized on technical grounds but rarely because they are suspected of being elements of the foreign policy of the United States. On the other hand, a true breakthrough may require a Marshall Plan approach rather than a project loan approach and in such an approach the giving nations will naturally expect to impose economic conditions.

Recently, it is said that the United States Government intends to place more emphasis on self-help as a criterion for extending assistance. If this is interpreted as requiring recipient countries to agree to carry out certain policies *of proved efficacy in promoting development,* well and good. But in this case, the United States must be as certain as it is possible to be that its requirements will actually accomplish the objective of making further assistance, after a reasonable period, no longer necessary. If, however, the criterion of self-help is interpreted as meaning that a country must have shown a commendable rate of "development" before qualifying for aid, the new policy may be disastrous. Referring to our analogy of the rehabilitation of individuals, it is the most demoralized and disorganized that are the greatest threats to society and are most in need of treatment.

It has also been said that recipient countries will be expected "to do something about the birth rate." This presumably means dissemination of family planning knowledge or the setting up of clinics for that purpose. This may or may not be efficacious, or possibly be sufficient in some countries but not in others. What we know to date suggests that a rise in the educational and economic levels is a necessary condition of a marked fall in birth rates. For instance there has, presumably, been no lack of birth control information in Puerto Rico for the past twenty and more years. The continuing high, though slowly falling, rate of population growth suggests that other causes, such as continued inequality and the persistence of substantial numbers of very poor people, especially in rural areas, may be an important factor. In a matter of such desperate urgency, policies should obviously be based on serious study and not wishful thinking.

The real difficulty here is that there is no consensus as yet on how to spark a breakthrough or even on whether a breakthrough is feasible and desirable. The various lending and advisory groups are still committed to the policies pursued over the past sixteen years, even though it is not difficult to show that these policies have not been successful. In essence they consist in trying to make individual projects better, to finance the foreign exchange requirements of such projects, and to add a bit to the total volume of national investment. When national overall policies are specifically offered, they either take a crude, highly over-simplified post-Keynesian form of increasing public investment, or urging (and even requiring) a greater measure of fiscal, monetary and exchange orthodoxy. Gardner Ackley, the Chairman of the Council of Economic Advisers, was recently quoted as saying, with commendable humility, that economists just don't know enough as yet about the conditions of full employment. With even greater justice his remark could be extended to the conditions of development. This, then, must be the first order of business. I have elsewhere suggested that we try out some new lines of attack in collaboration with willing pilot countries.[2] Due

2 Lauchlin Currie, *Accelerating Development: The Necessity and the Means* (New York: McGraw-Hill Book Co., 1966).

to the at least three different groupings into which underdeveloped countries fall, it would appear desirable that such controlled experiments be conducted in Latin America, Africa and S.E. Asia. If, as, and when the economic technicians have some reason to feel they have the answer, they will be in a position to let the developed countries know the cost of a once-and-for-all breakthrough Marshall Plan type operation on an international scale. We can then contrast this with the cost of an indefinite continuance of present policies plus the infinitely greater cost of failure and the consequences of a loss of control over environment on a continually growing scale.

To clear the way for a study of new approaches and controlled experiments three prerequisites appear to be necessary: a recognition that the present approach is failing in its basic end of creating viable economies, the abandonment of the gross national product per capita as an objective of policy and test of success and the adoption of more significant criteria, and a decision not to use foreign aid as an arm of foreign policy in the narrow sense of the term as used by Professor Morgenthau.

I would not for a moment minimize the extreme difficulty of the task. But I would also insist that the consequences of failure justify any effort. The verdict of the next generation on present leaders of developed countries will most certainly not be on the policies that most concern those leaders today but on their wisdom and foresight in discharging the awful responsibility that the present complete loss of control of man over his environment has thrust upon them.